Critical praise for the book

"[Merton] was a prophet whose writings foreshadowed many of the concerns and problems of living the spiritual life today . . . [This book contains] a selection for each day of the year, giving the reader the opportunity to begin or end each day with an insightful thought from one of Catholicism's most brilliant and prophetic figures."—*Clergy Book Service*

". . . an ideal introduction to the spirituality of this Cistercian monk and hermit."—*Spiritual Book News*

"Daybooks are for stimulation, overview and in-depth exposure to the mind, and in this case, heart of the author . . . Merton's thought covers a wide spectrum of interest. The reader needs to be ready for wonderful expressions of reverence for the simple and ordinary blessings of life. Sparked through the collection are flashes of pain, indignity, and deep humanity . . . By mixing Merton's musings of the church year and nature's calendar, the editor gives us 'pure Merton' with an honest sense of the man's life and its passions."—*Augsburg Book Newsletter*

"While some recent publications have had to glean from the edges of [Merton's] fields, this one collects from the center. It raids his writings for short passages, one a day, which can serve as lights and guides for those who walk in a world he knew from behind hermitage walls."
—*The Christian Century*

"Thoughtful readers will welcome Merton's wisdom and style . . . Sketches by the gifted Merton add to the pleasure of reading BLAZE OF RECOGNITION."—*Columbia*

"One of the greatest tributes that can be paid to a writer of religious themes is to assemble excerpts of his work as a year-long devotional guide . . . This book . . . deserves attention and can be used as an introduction to Merton's other works."—*The Courier-Journal*

"It is difficult to think of a better companion for the living of the days of a year than Thomas Merton."—*Sojourners*

"Trying to skim through this book all at one time can cause mental indigestion. It's that rich with thought-provoking statements."—*Charisma*

"The thoughts are brief and meaningful . . . Thoughts for good. Thoughts that key interest in deeper meanings and set your feet in right directions."—*The News Chief*

Through the Year
With
THOMAS MERTON
Daily Meditations from His Writings

Selected and edited by
THOMAS P. McDONNELL

with illustrations by
THOMAS MERTON

Originally published under the complete title:

BLAZE OF RECOGNITION
Through the Year with Thomas Merton:
Daily Meditations

IMAGE BOOKS
A Division of Doubleday & Company, Inc.
Garden City, New York
1985

Library of Congress Cataloging in Publication Data
Merton, Thomas, 1915–1968.
Through the year with Thomas Merton.
"Originally published under the complete title:
Blaze of recognition, through the year
with Thomas Merton, daily meditations."
1. Devotional calendars—Catholic Church.
2. Catholic Church—Prayer-books and
devotions—English.
I. McDonnell, Thomas P. II. Merton, Thomas, 1915–1968.
Blaze of recognition. III. Title.
BX2170.C56M48 1985   242′.2
Library of Congress Catalog Card Number: 85–11827
ISBN: 0-385-23234-9

Introduction

The quintessential Thomas Merton will always be, in my opinion, the Cistercian monk and contemplative whose locus of geography and spirit is irreversibly identified with the Abbey of Gethsemani in Kentucky. Though there was in Merton a certain restlessness of temperament that now and then tempted him to consider other regimens of the religious life and perhaps even to fantasize on new foundations in more or less esoteric places, it is the prayerful and meditative monk who remains central to the image we shall always have of him. In the end, as in the beginning, solitude was his only vocation.

The whole seeming paradox of Merton's vocation, however, was that out of this sense of solitude no monk or religious of our time had so thoroughly engaged the concerns, the perplexities, and the hopes in justice of the great world itself. Someone has said that Merton's idea of solitude was to pitch a tent—or, better still, to build a hermitage—in the middle of Times Square. The point is both amusing and contrary, for though Merton had ample gifts for the society of men and relished conversation with visitors to the Abbey of Gethsemani, especially when they were thoughtful enough to have brought beer along with them, and though he would sometimes play Bob Dylan records to rare and perhaps rarefied intellectuals like Jacques Maritain, who must have listened to this sort of music in a state of bemused astonishment, Merton had a very real capacity for true solitude.

The hermitage in Times Square, as an image for solitude at the noisy center of the world, must also remain slightly flawed when one considers the element that was present in everything Merton brought to a love of solitude—and that, of course, was his deep and abiding love of the natural world

around him. He lived a liturgy of the seasons as much as he
worshiped the seasons of the liturgy. The fact that this mutu-
ality happened to coincide perfectly with the Cistercian
tradition itself, I think, is what made him perhaps the most
memorable monk of our century. All the more amazing, he
was an American monk whose love of nature could not be
identified as a product of the romanticism of Emerson,
Thoreau, or Whitman, and which in our time has culminated
in the solipsism of, say, Wallace Stevens and others. Thomas
Merton's love of nature was purely sacramental, and in this
he is all but unique in American literature insofar as it expresses a religious and moral concern.

That is why, in these daily meditations from the writings
of Thomas Merton, a disproportionate number of the entries
reflect a constant awareness of the created world. It was to
be expected, too, that the majority of these selections would
be drawn from those books or writings by Merton which
most resemble the journal as an unconscious art form and
receptacle for the *pensée,* the meditative thought, or otherwise quietly perceptive observations for any given day—and
the days of Thomas Merton were all "given" days, or days as
gifts for living in a new light. As a writer, Merton had a
sententious style that is typical of the keepers of journals and
notebooks. If he did not have Emerson's almost Montaigne-
like gift of the aphorism, if he could not write sentences as
consistently clean as Thoreau's split blocks of maple, he had
a nevertheless arresting and recognizable style. That con-
summate craftsman Evelyn Waugh once faulted Merton for
a lack of elegance in his prose, but the monk as writer was
just as often sensuous, passionate, and altogether alive in his
own particular mode, or even in his various modes, of expression.

I have said that Merton was more sententious in the books
and writings derived more or less directly from his journals
—resulting preeminently, of course, in such works as *The
Sign of Jonas* (1953), *Conjectures of a Guilty Bystander*

(1966), and *New Seeds of Contemplation* (1962)—and it is no untoward coincidence that these works are among the great spiritual classics of our time. It is well known to students of the steadily increasing body of Merton criticism that he had once devised a chart or graph on which he evaluated some thirty of his books, ranging with the years of publication from 1944 through 1967, and that he rated each work in one of the following categories: "Awful," "Bad," "Poor," "Fair," "Good," "Better," and "Best." It is not untypical of the man that his self-evaluations are, in the most critical sense, solidly realistic. He was, relatively speaking, without the writer's egotistical capacity for vainglory. It was also typical of his character that no one book reached the "Best" category, and less than half achieved a "Better" rating, though he no doubt meant that those in the latter category actually represented his best efforts in a lifetime of writing.

As far as the controversial writings are concerned—by which I mean those he wrote as a peace activist, an advocate of civil rights and social justice, a Western monk in dialogue with the East, and simply as a very moral and authentic human being concerned about the advancement of the human condition everywhere—it is best to read Merton whole. These sometimes extraordinary set pieces or prose poems, such as "Original Child Bomb" (1962) and "A Signed Confession of Crimes Against the State" (1960), are filled with a connective tissue that cannot be separated from the contexts of their completed statements. Also, it is this controversial Merton who must await the cumulative evaluations of several more decades of study. Critically—and, for that matter, biographically as well—the last words on Merton have not yet been written. I think he would have preferred it that way—meaning, of course, that he should still remain as open-ended to us now as he was when the only thing absolutely certain about him was that he was one of the burnt men of God.

What remains, then, is the quintessential Merton we have

noted above, the monk as meditative writer, who is accessible to everyone now. The writer and musicologist John Howard Griffin, Merton's officially designated biographer who died before he could complete the assignment, said in an exquisite monograph or progress report on the subject, titled "In Search of Thomas Merton" (1971), that the eternally writing monk "literally meditated on paper." Nothing could more accurately describe the book we have attempted to present to the reader, here and now, fifteen years after the death of its inspiration. For this indeed is the book of a man who literally meditated on paper, who left us these lovely and enduring thoughts in the scrawled but neatly arranged marks we call the alphabet, and who saw the days and nights as renewable gifts of God incarnated in the human experience of creation itself.

Stoughton, Massachusetts
Ash Wednesday, 1983

Foreword

These meditations are musings upon questions that are, to me, relatively or even absolutely important. They do not always pretend to be final answers to final questions, nor do they even claim to face those questions in the most fundamental possible terms. But at least I can hope they are thoughts that, for better or for worse, mean something in my own life. They do not aim to include everything that life can possibly mean, nor do they take in a broad general view of all that matters. They are simply observations of a few things that seem to me to matter.

No Man Is an Island

The purpose of a book of meditations is to teach you how to think and not to do your thinking for you. Consequently, if you pick up such a book and simply read it through, you are wasting your time. As soon as any thought stimulates your mind or heart, you can put the book down because your meditation has begun. To think that you are somehow obliged to follow the author of the book to his own particular conclusion would be a great mistake. It may happen that his conclusion does not apply to you. God may want you to end up somewhere else. He may have planned to give you quite a different grace from the one the author suggests you might need.

New Seeds of Contemplation

THROUGH THE YEAR WITH THOMAS MERTON

January

JANUARY 1

New Year's Day

Bells are meant to remind us that God alone is good, that we belong to him, that we are not living for this world.

They break in upon our cares in order to remind us that all things pass away and that our preoccupations are not important.

They speak to us of freedom, which responsibilities and transient cares make us forget.

They are the voice of our alliance with the God of heaven.

They tell us that we are his true temple. They call us to peace with him within ourselves.

The Gospel of Mary and Martha is read at the end of the Blessing of a Church Bell in order to remind us of all these things.

The bells say: business does not matter. Rest in God and rejoice, for this world is only the figure and the promise of a world to come, and only those who are detached from transient things can possess the substance of eternal promise.

The bells say: we have spoken for centuries from the towers of great churches. We have spoken to the saints, your fathers, in their land. We called them, as we call you, to sanctity.

—Thoughts in Solitude

JANUARY 2

A Change of Context

As long as I assume that the world is something I discover by turning on the radio or looking out the window, I am deceived from the start. As long as I imagine that the world is something to be "escaped from" in a monastery—that wearing a special costume and following a quaint observance take me "out of this world," I am dedicating my life to an illusion. Of course, I hasten to qualify this. I said a moment ago that, in a certain historic context of thought and of life, this kind of thought and action once made perfect sense. But the moment you change the context, then the whole thing has to be completely transposed. Otherwise, you are left like the orchestra in the Marx Brothers' *A Night at the Opera*, where Harpo had inserted "Take Me Out to the Ball Game" in the middle of the operatic score.

—Contemplation in a World of Action

JANUARY 3

Twilight of Dawn

We are like a bunch of drunken men at the last end of a long stupid party, falling over the furniture in the twilight of dawn.

—Seeds of Destruction

JANUARY 4

The Road Ahead

My Lord God, I have no idea where I am going, I do not see the road ahead of me, I cannot know for certain where it will end. Nor do I really know myself, and the fact that I think I am following your will does not mean that I am actually doing so. But I believe that the desire to please you does in fact please you. And I hope I have that desire in all that I am doing. I hope that I will never do anything apart from that desire. And I know that if I do this you will lead me by the right road, though I may know nothing about it. Therefore, I will trust you always, though I may seem to be lost and in the shadow of death. I will not fear, for you are ever with me, and you will never leave me to face my perils alone.

—*Thoughts in Solitude*

JANUARY 5

A Need for Mercy

Only the man who has had to face despair is really convinced that he needs mercy.

—*No Man Is an Island*

JANUARY 6

Thinking Men

Thinking men. Better still, *right-thinking* men! Who are they? . . . The right-thinking men are managers, leaders, but not eggheads. Hence they can be believed. They can justify any wrong road, and make it seem the only road. They can justify everything, even the destruction of the world.

—*Conjectures of a Guilty Bystander*

JANUARY 7

An Angry Man

A temperamentally angry man may be more inclined to anger than another. But as long as he remains sane he is still free not to be angry. His inclination to anger is simply a force in his character which can be turned to good or evil, according to his desires. If he desires what is evil, his temper will become a weapon of evil against other men and even against his own soul. If he desires what is good, his temper can become the controlled instrument for fighting the evil that is in himself and thus helping other men to overcome the obstacles which they meet in the world. He remains free to desire either good or evil.

—Thoughts in Solitude

A Zombie?

Man is all ready to become a god, and instead he appears at times to be a zombie.

—Conjectures of a Guilty Bystander

JANUARY 8

The Cult of Unoriginality

We are beginning to understand that we live in a climate of all-embracing conformities. We have become mass-produced automatons. Our lives, our homes, our cities, our thoughts, or perhaps our lack of thoughts, have all taken on an impersonal mask of resigned and monotonous sameness. We who once made such a cult of originality, experiment, personal commitment and individual creativity, now find ourselves among the least individual, the least original and least personal of all the people on the face of the earth . . . People "express themselves" in ways that grow more and more frantic in proportion as they realize that the individuality and the distinctive differences they are attempting to express no longer exist. . . . There is nothing so monotonously unoriginal as the capricious eccentricities of atoms in a mass-society.

—Seasons of Celebration

JANUARY 9

A Serious Birthday

On my forty-sixth birthday they put an ape into space. They shot him farther than they intended. . . . Let's be quite serious. Civilization has deigned to grace my forty-sixth birthday with this marvelous feat, and I should get ribald about it? Let me learn from this contented ape. . . . He did not complain of space. He did not complain of time. He did not complain either of earth or heaven.

—Conjectures of a Guilty Bystander

JANUARY 10

The Solitary View

The solitary is, first of all, one who renounces arbitrary social imagery. When his nation wins a war or sends a rocket to the moon, he can get along without feeling as if he personally had won the war or hit the moon with a rocket. When his nation is rich and arrogant, he does not feel that he himself is more fortunate and more honest, as well as more powerful, than the citizens of other, more "backward" nations. More than this, he is able to despise war and to see the futility of rockets to the moon in a way quite different and more fundamental from the way in which society may tolerate these negative views. That is to say, he despises the criminal, bloodthirsty arrogance of his own nation or class as much as that of "the enemy." He despises his own self-

seeking aggressivity as much as that of the politicians who
hypocritically pretend they are fighting for peace.
—*Disputed Questions*

JANUARY 11
A Pharisee

A pharisee is a righteous man whose righteousness is nourished by the blood of sinners.
—*Conjectures of a Guilty Bystander*

JANUARY 12
Peak of Intensity

We cannot be happy if we expect to live all the time at the
highest peak of intensity. Happiness is not a matter of intensity, but of balance and order and rhythm and harmony.
—*No Man Is an Island*

JANUARY 13
The Madding Crowd

Descending into the crowd, the individual loses his personality and his character and perhaps even his moral dignity as a human being. Contempt for the "crowd" is by no
means contempt for mankind. The crowd is below man. The
crowd devours the human that is in us to make us the mem-
bers of a many-headed beast. That is why the monastery
builds itself in the wilderness: cuts off communications with
the world, and with the press and the radio, which too often

are simply the voice of the vast aggregation that is something less than human. As a specialized, spiritual society, the monastic community must take care to form itself carefully in the atmosphere of solitude and detachment in which the seeds of faith and charity have a chance to sink deep roots and grow without being choked out by thorns, or crushed under the wheels of trucks and cars.

—*The Silent Life*

JANUARY 14

Every Moment

Every moment and every event of every man's life on earth plants something in his soul.

—*New Seeds of Contemplation*

JANUARY 15

Definitions of Prayer

Prayer is freedom and affirmation growing out of nothingness into love. Prayer is the flowering of our inmost freedom, in response to the Word of God. Prayer is not only dialogue with God: it is the communication of our freedom with his ultimate freedom, his infinite spirit. It is the elevation of our limited freedom into the infinite freedom of the divine spirit and of the divine love. Prayer is the encounter of our freedom with the all-embracing charity which knows no limit and knows no obstacle. Prayer is an emergence into this area of infinite freedom. Prayer, then, is not an abject procedure, though sometimes it may spring from our abjection. But prayer is not something that is meant to maintain us in servility and helplessness. We take stock of our own wretch-

edness at the beginning of prayer in order to rise beyond it
and above it to infinite freedom and infinite creative love in
God.

—Contemplation in a World of Action

A Time for Contemplation

O God, do not let me take away from you the time that
belongs to you in contemplation.

—The Sign of Jonas

JANUARY 16

Resolution

Keep your eyes clean and your ears quiet and your mind
serene. Breathe God's air. Work, if you can, under his sky.

—New Seeds of Contemplation

JANUARY 17

Moments of Rest

In the interior life there should be moments of relaxation,
freedom, and "browsing." Perhaps the best way to do this is
in the midst of nature, but also in literature. Perhaps, also, a
certain amount of art is necessary, and music. Of course, we
have to remember our time is limited and first things have to
come first. We can't spend too much time just listening to
music.

You also need a good garden, and you need access to the
woods, or to the sea. Get out in those hills and really be in the
midst of nature a little bit! That is not only legitimate, it is in

a certain way necessary. Don't take your cloister concept too materially. Now, I may be running into all kinds of problems with constitutions. But the woods and nature should be part of your solitude, and if it's not periodically part of your solitude, I think the law should be changed.

—*Contemplation in a World of Action*

JANUARY 18
Sanity of Solitude

The one great advantage of the woods is that one cannot— at least sanely—play a part in them. Or if one manages to defy reality and continue in some fictitious "role," the result will quickly prove disastrous. At the same time, it is not altogether easy to be perfectly honest with oneself, and solitude brings this fact out. The woods may well foment new madnesses that one did not suspect before. But it would seem that solitude is not a satisfactory setting for concerted, thoroughgoing madness. To be really mad you need other people.

When you are by yourself, you soon get tired of your craziness. It is too exhausting. It does not fit in with the eminent sanity of trees, birds, water, sky. You have to shut up and go about the business of living. The silence of the woods forces you to make a decision which the tensions and artificialities of society may help you evade forever. Do you want to be yourself or don't you? . . . Are you going to stand on your own feet before God and the world and take full responsibility for your own life?

—*Contemplation in a World of Action*

JANUARY 19

A Symbolic Figure

We must remember that Robinson Crusoe was one of the great myths of the middle-class, commercial civilization of the eighteenth and nineteenth centuries: the myth not of eremitical solitude but of pragmatic individualism. Crusoe is a symbolical figure in an era when every man's house was his castle in the trees, but only because every man was a very prudent and resourceful citizen who knew how to make the best out of the least and could drive a hard bargain with a competitor, even with life itself. Carefree Crusoe was happy because he had an answer to everything. The real hermit is not so sure he has an answer.

—Disputed Questions

JANUARY 20

False Sweetness

When you are led by God into the darkness where contemplation is found, you are not able to rest in the false sweetness of your own will. The fake interior satisfaction of self-complacency and absolute confidence in your own judgment will never be able to deceive you entirely: it will make you slightly sick, and you will be forced by a vague sense of interior nausea to gash yourself open and let the poison out.

—New Seeds of Contemplation

JANUARY 21
Guided by Nobody

The most dangerous man in the world is the contemplative who is guided by nobody. He trusts his own visions. He obeys the attractions of an interior voice, but will not listen to other men. He identifies the will of God with anything that makes him feel, within his own heart, a big, warm, sweet interior glow. The sweeter and the warmer the feeling, the more he is convinced of his own infallibility. And if the sheer force of his own self-confidence communicates itself to other people and gives them the impression that he is really a saint, such a man can wreck a whole city, or a religious order, or even a nation. The world is covered with the scars that have been left in its flesh by visionaries like these. However, very often these people are nothing more than harmless bores.

—New Seeds of Contemplation

JANUARY 22
Giving Advice

It is our innocence to die without argument. People ask me advice. I suppose I shouldn't give it. I feel terrible when I do—not because they will think I am a fool, but because they might go ahead and take it.

—The Sign of Jonas

JANUARY 23

The Wise Heart

I pray much to have a wise heart, and perhaps the rediscovery of Lady Julian of Norwich will help me. I took her book with me on a quiet walk among the cedars. She is a true theologian with greater clarity, depth, and order than Saint Teresa: she really elaborates, theologically, the content of her revelations. She first experienced, then thought, and the thoughtful deepening of her experience worked it back into her life, deeper and deeper, until her whole life as a recluse at Norwich was simply a matter of getting completely saturated in the light she had received all at once, in the "shewings," when she thought she was going to die.

One of her most telling and central convictions is her orientation to what might be called an *eschatological secret,* the hidden dynamism which is at work already and by which "all manner of thing shall be well." To have a "wise heart," it seems to me, is to live centered on this dynamism and this secret hope—this hoped-for secret.

The wise heart lives in Christ.

—Conjectures of a Guilty Bystander

JANUARY 24

The Devil Preaching

The devil is not afraid to preach the will of God, provided he can preach it in his own way.

—New Seeds of Contemplation

JANUARY 25

Dante's Vision

Man has lost Dante's vision of that "love which moves the sun and other stars," and in so doing he has lost the power to find meaning in his world. Not that he has not been able to understand the physical world better. The disappearance of the simple medieval cosmogony upon which Dante built his structure of hell, purgatory, and heaven has enabled man to break out of the limitations imposed upon his science by that ancient conception. And now he is prepared to fly out into those depths of space which terrified Pascal—and which continue to terrify anyone who is still human. Yet, though man has acquired the power to do almost anything, he has at the same time lost the ability to orient his life toward a spiritual goal by the things that he does. He has lost all conviction that he knows where he is going and what he is doing, unless he can manage to plunge into some collective delusion which promises happiness (sometime in the future) to those who will have learned to use the implements he has discovered.

—Disputed Questions

JANUARY 26

Bernards and Abelards

The Bernards and Abelards of our time will be, perhaps, not people but machines: great, brilliant, temperamental computers. One of these days the most brilliant computer will take offense. Then watch!

—Conjectures of a Guilty Bystander

JANUARY 27

Like a Skyrocket

Mental prayer is something like a skyrocket. Kindled by a spark of divine love, the soul streaks heavenward in an act of intelligence as clear and direct as the rocket's trail of fire. Grace has released all the deepest energies of our spirit and assists us to climb to new and unsuspected heights. Nevertheless, our own faculties soon reach their limit. The intelligence can climb no higher into the sky. There is a point where the mind bows down its fiery trajectory as if to acknowledge its limitations and proclaim the infinite supremacy of the unattainable God.

But it is here that our "meditation" reaches its climax. Love again takes the initiative, and the rocket "explodes" in a burst of sacrificial praise. Thus love flings out a hundred burning stars, acts of all kinds, expressing everything that is best in man's spirit, and the soul spends itself in drifting fires that glorify the name of God, while they fall earthward and die away in the night wind!

—*Spiritual Direction and Meditation*

JANUARY 28

In This Night

If a man in this night lets his spirit get carried away with fear or impatience and anxiety, he will come to a standstill. He will twist and turn and torture himself with attempts to see some light and feel some warmth and recapture the old consolations that are beyond recovery.

—*New Seeds of Contemplation*

JANUARY 29

An Ordinary Human Being

True Christian "openness to the world" proceeds from a genuine respect for being and for man, and for man's natural and historical setting in the world.

What is the good of exalting the "greatness of man" simply because the concerted efforts of technicians, soldiers, and politicians manage to put a man on the moon while four-fifths of the human race remain in abject misery, not properly clothed or fed, in lives subject to arbitrary and senseless manipulation by politicians or to violence at the hands of police, hoodlums, or revolutionaries?

Certainly, the possibilities and the inherent nobility of man are stupendous: but it is small help to crow about it when the celebration of his theoretic greatness does nothing to help him find himself as an ordinary human being.

—*Conjectures of a Guilty Bystander*

JANUARY 30

A Need for Truth

Man today has lost consciousness of his need for truth. What he seeks is power. Truth is made to serve the ends of power. Truth is of no value unless it is expedient. When truth is not expedient, then it is deliberately manipulated and twisted to serve the aims of the powerful. Objective truth is considered irrelevant. It is derided by the powerful, who can change truth to suit themselves, and bend it this way and that for the sake of ambition and fortune.

—*Seasons of Celebration*

January 31

Tainted with Poison

We must be wary of ourselves when the worst that is in man becomes objectified in society, approved, acclaimed and deified, when hatred becomes patriotism and murder a holy duty, when spying and delation are called love of truth and the stool pigeon is a public benefactor, when the gnawing and prurient resentments of frustrated bureaucrats become the conscience of the people and the gangster is enthroned in power, then we must fear the voice of our own heart, even when it denounces them. For are we not all tainted with the same poison?

—Emblems of a Season of Fury

Our Naked Realities

We cling to our eccentricities and our selfishness, but we do so in a way that is no longer interesting because it is, after all, mechanical and vulgar.

—The Sign of Jonas

February

FEBRUARY 1

A Dying World

Most of the world is either asleep or dead. The religious people are, for the most part, asleep. The irreligious are dead. Those who are asleep are divided into two classes, like the Virgins in the parable, waiting for the Bridegroom's coming. The wise have oil in their lamps. That is to say, they are detached from themselves and from the cares of the world, and they are full of charity. They are indeed waiting for the Bridegroom, and they desire nothing else but his coming, even though they may fall asleep while waiting for him to appear. But the others are not only asleep: they are full of other dreams and other desires. Their lamps are empty because they have burned themselves out in the wisdom of the flesh and in their own vanity. When he comes, it is too late for them to buy oil. They light their lamps only after he has gone. So they fall asleep again, with useless lamps, and when they wake up they trim them to investigate, once again, the matters of a dying world.

—*No Man Is an Island*

FEBRUARY 2

A Stranger to Myself

If a man has to be pleasing to me, comforting, reassuring, before I can love him, then I cannot truly love him. Not that love cannot console or reassure! But if I demand first to be reassured, I will never dare to begin loving. If a man has to be a Jew or a Christian before I can love him, then I cannot love him. If he has to be black or white before I can love him, then I cannot love him. If he has to belong to my political party or social group before I can love him, if he has to wear any kind of uniform, then my love is no longer love because it is not free: it is dictated by something outside itself. It is dominated by an appetite other than love. I love not the person but his classification, and in that event I love him not as a person but as a thing. In this way I remain at the mercy of forces outside myself, and those who seem to me to be neighbors are indeed strangers; for I am, first of all, a stranger to myself.

—Seasons of Celebration

FEBRUARY 3

Conscience

Conscience is the face of the soul.

—No Man Is an Island

FEBRUARY 4

In Deep Solitude

It is in deep solitude that I find the gentleness with which I can truly love my brothers. The more solitary I am, the more affection I have for them. It is pure affection, and filled with reverence for the solitude of others. Solitude and silence teach me to love my brothers for what they are, not for what they say. Now it is no longer a question of dishonoring them by accepting their fictions, believing in their image of themselves, which their weakness obliges them to compose, in the wan work of communication. Yet there will, it is true, always remain a dialectic between the words of men and

their being. This will tell something about them we would
not have realized if the words had not been there.

—The Sign of Jonas

FEBRUARY 5

A Refusal to Love

Beware of the temptation to refuse love, to reject love, for
ostensibly "spiritual motives." Consider the awful sterility of
those who, claiming to love God, have in reality dispensed
themselves from all obligations to love anyone, and have
remained inert and stunted in a little circle of abstract, petty
concerns involving themselves and a few others as sterile as
themselves!

—Conjectures of a Guilty Bystander

FEBRUARY 6

The Narrow Limit

It was utterly beautiful out there in the snow this afternoon. Everything was blue. Plenty of snow in the branches
of the cedars, but it was melting fast in the sun. Before
Vespers, the shoulders of the hills were brown. But it was
beautifully quiet except, for a moment, I could hear what
might have been bombers, but not bombs or guns.

Why do I desire things that are not God?

Inside me, I quickly come to the barrier, the limit of what
I am, beyond which I cannot go by myself. It is such a narrow
limit, and yet for years I thought it was the universe. Now I
see it is nothing. If I never become anything but a writer,
that is what it will amount to—sitting on my own desert
island, which is not much bigger than an English penny.

How quickly my limits accuse me of my nothingness, and I cannot go beyond. I pause and reflect, and reflection makes it more final. Then I forget to reflect anymore, and by surprise I make a little escape, at least to the threshold, and love moves in darkness, just enough to tell me that there is such a thing as freedom.

—The Sign of Jonas

FEBRUARY 7

An Easy Virtue

Some men are only virtuous enough to forget that they are sinners, without being wretched enough to remember how much they need the mercy of God.

—No Man Is an Island

FEBRUARY 8

Doing Great Things

There are men dedicated to God whose lives are full of restlessness and who have no real desire to be alone. Interior solitude is impossible for them. They fear it. They do everything they can to escape it. What is worse, they try to draw everyone else into activities as senseless and as devouring as their own. They are great promoters of useless work. They love to organize meetings and banquets and conferences and lectures. They print circulars, write letters, talk for hours on the telephone in order that they may gather a hundred people together in a large room where they will all fill the air with smoke and make a great deal of noise and roar at one another and clap their hands and stagger home at last, patting one another on the back with the assurance that they have all done great things to spread the Kingdom of God.

—New Seeds of Contemplation

Wearing Our Mitres

Let us examine our consciences, brethren: do we wear our mitres even to bed? I am afraid we sometimes do.

—Conjectures of a Guilty Bystander

FEBRUARY 9

Dangerous Ambiguities

As a nation, we have begun to float off into a moral void, and all the sermons of all the priests in the country (if they preach at all) are not going to help much. We have got to the point where the promulgation of any kind of moral standard automatically releases an anti-moral response in a whole lot of people. It is not with them, above all, that I am concerned, but with the "good" people, the right-thinking people, who stick to principle, all right, except where it conflicts with the chance to make money. It seems to me that there are very dangerous ambiguities about our democracy in its actual present condition. I wonder to what extent our ideals are now a front for organized selfishness and systematic irresponsibility. If our affluent society ever breaks down and the facade is taken away, what are we going to have left?

—Seeds of Destruction

FEBRUARY 10

Light of the World

We are supposed to be the light of the world. We are supposed to be a light to ourselves and to others. That may well be what accounts for the fact that the world is in darkness!

—Life and Holiness

FEBRUARY 11

God's Paradox

No escape from paradox: Wisdom manifests itself, and is yet hidden. The more it hides, the more it is manifest; and the more it is manifest, the more it is hidden. For God is known when he is apprehended as unknown, and he is heard when we realize that we do not know the sound of his voice. The words he utters are words full of silence, and they are bait to draw us into silence. The truths he manifests are full of hiddenness, and their function is to hide us, with themselves, in God from whom they proceed. If we hide the precepts of his wisdom in our heart—precepts of humility, meekness, charity, renunciation, faith, prayer—they themselves will hide us in him. For the values which these virtues communicate to us, the life which they give to us, are completely hidden from the eyes of men. They bring us to the source of a life that is unknown to the natural wisdom of man, and yet from this source man's nature itself proceeds, is nourished, and is sustained.

—Seasons of Celebration

Perfect Praise

I will hold to the saying that: "Perfect joy is to be without joy. Perfect praise is to be without praise."

—The Way of Chuang Tzu

FEBRUARY 12

Ash Wednesday

Gray skies. It rained in the night. The lights all went out at ten to two, and we said Matins and the Office of the Dead and Lauds and Prime with many candles. The flu has not left me, and my head is full of glue and I can't breathe.

And yet Ash Wednesday is full of joy. In a minute we will sing None and go barefoot to get ashes on our heads to remember, with great relief, that we are dust. The source of all sorrow is the illusion that of ourselves we are anything but dust. God is all our joy and in him our dust can become splendor. The great sorrow of mankind is turned to joy by the love of Christ, and the secret of happiness is no longer to see any sorrow except in the light of Christ's victory over sorrow. And then all sorrow contributes somehow to our happiness.

Thus I sit here in the corner of the upstairs Scriptorium and look out the window at the bare trees in the préau and the gray guesthouse wall and at my own little happy corner of the sky.

—The Sign of Jonas

FEBRUARY 13

On Fasting

Fasting is a good thing because food itself is a good thing. But the good things of this world have this about them, that they are good in their season and not out of it. Food is good, but to be constantly eating is a bad thing—and, in fact, it is not even pleasant. The man who gorges himself with food and drink enjoys his surfeiting much less than the fasting person enjoys his frugal collation.

Even the fast itself, in moderation and according to God's will, is a pleasant thing. There are healthy natural joys in self-restraint: joys of the spirit, which shares its lightness even with the flesh. Happy is the man whose flesh does not burden his spirit, but rests only lightly upon its arm, like a graceful companion.

—Seasons of Celebration

An Unfree Person

No man who simply eats and drinks whenever he feels like eating and drinking, who smokes whenever he feels the urge to light a cigarette, who gratifies his curiosity and sensuality whenever they are stimulated, can consider himself a free person.

—New Seeds of Contemplation

FEBRUARY 14

Love of Ourselves

If you discover any kind of love that satiates you, it is not the end for which you were created. Any act that can cease to be a joy is not the end of your existence. If you grow tired of a love that you thought was the love of God, be persuaded that what you are tired of was never pure love, but either some act ordered to that love or else something without order altogether.

The one love that always grows weary of its object and is never satiated with anything and is always looking for something different and new is the love of ourselves. It is the source of all boredom and all restlessness and all unquiet and all misery and all unhappiness—ultimately, it is hell.

—*The Waters of Siloe*

FEBRUARY 15
Humanistic Love

Humanistic love will not serve. As long as we believe that we hate no one, that we are merciful, that we are kind by our very nature, we deceive ourselves; our hatred is merely smoldering under the gray ashes of complacent optimism. We are apparently at peace with everyone because we think we are worthy. We have lost the capacity to face the question of unworthiness at all. But when we are delivered by the mercy of God, the question no longer has a meaning.

—*New Seeds of Contemplation*

FEBRUARY 16
Purification

The greatest need of our time is to clean out the enormous mass of mental and emotional rubbish that clutters our minds and makes of all political and social life a mass illness. Without this housecleaning we cannot begin to see. Unless we see, we cannot think. The purification must begin with the mass media. How?

—*Conjectures of a Guilty Bystander*

All That Glitters

Our minds are like crows. They pick up everything that

glitters, no matter how uncomfortable our nests get with all the metal in them.

—New Seeds of Contemplation

FEBRUARY 17

A Serious Person

A great deal of virtue and piety is simply the easy price we pay in order to justify a life that is essentially trifling. Nothing is so cheap as the evasion purchased by just enough good conduct to make one pass as a "serious person."

—Conjectures of a Guilty Bystander

Epitaph

Here lies a dead man who made an idol of indifference. His prayer did not enkindle, it extinguished his flame.

His silence listened to nothing and, therefore, heard nothing, and had nothing to say.

Let the swallows come and build their nests in his history and teach their young to fly about in the desert which he made of his soul, and thus he will not remain unprofitable forever.

—No Man Is an Island

FEBRUARY 18

Death in Ourselves

The Persian Sufi poet Rumi (thirteenth century) writes this about death, showing that our attitude toward death is in reality a reflection of our own attitude toward ourself and toward our life. He who truly loves life—and lives it—is able to accept death without sorrow.

Rumi's poem is on "The Beauty of Death." It reads in part: Everyone's death is of the same quality as himself, my son: to the enemy of God an enemy, to the friend of God a friend . . .

Your fear of death is really fear of yourself: see what it is from which you are fleeing!

'Tis your own ugly face, not the visage of death: your spirit is like the tree, death like the leaf.

Yet this "friendship" with death is not the same as a pathological deathwish. The deathwish is merely a refusal of life, an abdication from the difficulties and sorrows of living, a resentment of its joys. The deathwish is an incapacity for life. True acceptance of death in freedom and faith demands a mature and fruitful acceptance of life. He who fears death or who longs for it—both are in the same condition: they admit they have not lived.

—Conjectures of a Guilty Bystander

FEBRUARY 19

Ultimate Purpose

No matter how ruined man and his world may seem to be, and no matter how terrible man's despair may become, as long as he continues to be a man his very humanity continues to tell him that life has a meaning. That, indeed, is one reason why man tends to rebel against himself. If he could without effort see what the meaning of life is, and if he could fulfill his ultimate purpose without trouble, he would never question the fact that life is well worth living. Or if he saw at once that life had no purpose and no meaning, the question would never arise. In either case, man would not be capable of finding himself so much of a problem.

—No Man Is an Island

FEBRUARY 20
An Age of Bad Dreams

We live in an age of bad dreams, in which the scientist and engineer possess the power to give external form to the phantasms of man's unconscious. The bright weapons that sing in the atmosphere, ready to pulverize the cities of the world, are the dreams of giants without a center. Their mathematical evolutions are hieratic rites devised by shamans without belief. One is permitted to wish their dreams had been less sordid!

—Emblems of a Season of Fury

FEBRUARY 21
Innocent Without Sorrow

Evening: cold winter wind along the walls of the chapel. Not howling, not moaning, not dismal. Can there be anything mournful about the wind? It is innocent and without sorrow. It has no regrets. Wind is a strong child enjoying his play, amazed at his own strength, gentle, inexhaustible, and pure. He burnishes the dry snow, throwing clouds of it against the building. The wind has no regrets. The chapel is very cold. The two die-hard novices remain there alone, kneeling both upright, very still, no longer even pretending to enjoy or to understand anything.

—Conjectures of a Guilty Bystander

FEBRUARY 22
Human Nature

Human nature is not evil. All pleasure is not wrong. All spontaneous desires not selfish. The doctrine of original sin does not mean that human nature has been completely corrupted and that man's freedom is always inclined to sin. Man is neither a devil nor an angel. He is not a pure spirit, but a being of flesh and spirit, subject to error and malice, but basically inclined to seek truth and goodness. He is, indeed, a sinner: but his heart responds to love and grace. It also responds to the goodness and to the need of his fellowman.

—*Life and Holiness*

FEBRUARY 23

Alone with God

The man who fears to be alone will never be anything but lonely, no matter how much he may surround himself with people. But the man who learns, in solitude and recollection, to be at peace with his own loneliness, and to prefer its reality to the illusion of merely natural companionship, comes to know the invisible companionship of God. Such a one is alone with God in all places, and he alone truly enjoys the companionship of other men, because he loves them in God, in whom their presence is not tiresome, and because of whom his own love for them can never know satiety.

—*No Man Is an Island*

FEBRUARY 24

On Suffering Alone

When a man suffers, he is most alone. Therefore, it is in suffering that we are most tested as persons. How can we face the awful interior questioning? What shall we answer when we come to be examined by pain? Without God, we are no longer persons. We lose our manhood and our dignity.

34

We become dumb animals and die without too much commotion. Suffering is wasted, if we suffer entirely alone.

—*No Man Is an Island*

FEBRUARY 25

Spiritual Pride

And now I am thinking of the disease which is spiritual pride. I am thinking of the peculiar unreality that gets into the hearts of the saints and eats their sanctity away before it matures. There is something of this worm in the hearts of all religious men. This sickness is most dangerous when it succeeds in looking like humility. When a proud man thinks he is humble, his case is hopeless. Having become a martyr, he is ten times as stubborn as before.

It is a terrible thing when such a one gets the idea he is a prophet or a messenger of God or a man with a mission to reform the world. He is capable of destroying religion and making the name of God odious to men.

—*New Seeds of Contemplation*

FEBRUARY 26

Love of Power

The man who loves power can, with most idealistic motives, seek to gratify this love not only by exercising his power over his contemporaries but even by building his will into the structure of the institution, so that later generations will go on being dominated by him long after his death.

—*Contemplation in a World of Action*

Our Own Measure

Every one of us forms an idea of Christ that is limited and incomplete. It is cut according to our own measure.

—New Seeds of Contemplation

FEBRUARY 27

Land of the Beloved

The song of my Beloved beside the stream. The birds descanting in their clerestories. His skies have sanctified my eyes, His woods are clearer than the King's palace. But the air and I will never tell our secret.

Christ has sanctified the desert, and in the desert I discovered it. The woods have all become young in the discipline of the spring: but it is the discipline of expectancy only. Which one cut more keenly? The February sunlight, or the air? There are no buds. Buds are not guessed at, or thought of, this early in Lent. But the wilderness shines with promise. The land is dressed in simplicity and strength. Everything foretells the coming of the holy spring. I had never before spoken so freely or so intimately with woods, hills, birds, water, and sky. On this great day, however, they understood their position and they remained mute in the presence of the Beloved. Only his light was obvious and eloquent. My brother and sister, the light and water. The stump and the stone. The tables of rock. The blue, naked sky. Tractor tracks, a little waterfall. And Mediterranean solitude. I thought of Italy after my Beloved had spoken and was gone.

—The Sign of Jonas

FEBRUARY 28/29

Human Aspiration

The terrible human aspiration that reaches out over the abyss is calmed. The terror of God is so far beyond all conceivable terror that it ceases to terrify, and then suddenly becomes friendly. Then, at last, begins the utterly unbelievable consolation, the consolation into which we enter through the door of apparent despair: the deep conviction, as impossible to explain as it is to resist, that in the depths of our uselessness and futility we are one with God. "He who is joined to the Lord is one spirit." We have found him in the abyss of our own poverty—not in a horrible night, not in a tragic immolation, but simply in the ordinary, uninteresting actuality of our own everyday life.

—Seasons of Celebration

The Truest Solitude

The truest solitude is not something outside you, not an absence of men or of sound around you: it is an abyss opening up in the center of your own soul.

And this abyss of interior solitude is a hunger that will never be satisfied with any created thing.

The only way to find solitude is by hunger and thirst and sorrow and poverty and desire. The man who has found solitude is empty, as if he had been emptied by death.

—New Seeds of Contemplation

March

MARCH 1

This Gay, Windy Month

I enter into this gay, windy month with my mind full of the Book of Josue. Its battle scenes are like the Bayeux tapestry. The books of the Old Testament become to us as signs of the zodiac, and Josue (somewhere near the spring equinox) stands at the opposite side of heaven from Job (where all the sky is sailing down to darkness).

Here is a book for spring. The sap is rising in the trees, and the children of God are winning all their battles. And it is Lent, when Josue (our Christ) calls the five captive kings, cowering from their cave, and makes his officers put their feet upon their necks. Then the five kings go to the gibbet. That is what Jesus makes us do to the five senses in Lent.

Josue is a conqueror and even a poet. He lifted up his head in the heat of battle and sang a two-line poem to the sun and moon, and both stood still. For the sun did not go down toward Gabaon nor the moon to the valley of Ajalon. Even so, Christ has delayed the Day of Judgment, giving us time to do penance.

—The Sign of Jonas

MARCH 2

Man on the Brink

The world of our time is in confusion. It is reaching the peak of the greatest crisis in history. Never before has there been such a total upheaval of the whole human race. Tremendous forces are at work: spiritual, sociological, economic, technological and, least of all, political. Mankind

stands on the brink of a new barbarism, yet at the same time
there remain possibilities for an unexpected and almost unbelievable solution, the creation of a new world and a new
civilization, the like of which has never been seen. We are
face to face either with Antichrist or the Millennium, no one
knows which.

—*The Silent Life*

MARCH 3

Self-Hatred

The history of our own time has been made by dictators
whose characters, often transparently easy to read, have
been full of repressed guilt, self-hatred, and feelings of infe-
riority. They have managed to enlist the support of solid
masses of men moved by the same repressed drives as themselves. The wars they have waged with one another have
been the sacrifice which the masses, degraded by totalitarianism, have offered up in fanatical self-idolatry, which never
completely manages to assuage the nausea brought about by
self-hatred.

—*The Living Bread*

MARCH 4

Flight from God

The whole mechanism of modern life is geared for a flight
from God and from the spirit into the wilderness of neurosis.

—*No Man Is an Island*

MARCH 5

The Deadly Game

Lanza del Vasto noted a deep connection between *play* and *war*, even before the games theory and nuclear war strategy became practically identified. In our society, everything, in fact, is a game. But if everything is a game, then everything leads to war. Play is aimless and yet multiplies obstacles so that the "aim," which in fact does not exist, cannot be attained by the opponent. For instance, getting a ball in the hole.

War is caused by similar aimless aims. Not by hunger, not by real need. War is a game of the powerful, or of whole collectivities devoted to self-assertion. It is "the great public vice that consists in playing with the lives of other men." War plays with life and death, and does so magnificently. Everybody becomes involved. Everybody has to live or die —so that the other side may not get a ball in the hole. But the real excitement of the game comes from the suspension of conscience. In all play, one has to prescind from real conditions.

—*Conjectures of a Guilty Bystander*

MARCH 6

Independent Voices

In an age when totalitarianism has striven, in every way, to devaluate and degrade the human person, we hope it is right to demand a hearing for any and every sane reaction in favor of man's inalienable solitude and his interior freedom. The murderous din of our materialism cannot be allowed to silence the independent voices which will never cease to speak, whether they are the voice of Christian saints, or the voices of Oriental sages like Lao-Tse or the Zen masters, or the voices of men like Thoreau or Martin Buber, or Max Picard. It is all very well to insist that man is a "social animal" —the fact is obvious enough. But that is no justification for making him a mere cog in a totalitarian machine—or in a religious one either, for that matter.

—Thoughts in Solitude

MARCH 7

Closing Their Eyes

The experience of twentieth-century dictatorships has shown that it is possible for some Christians to live and work in a shockingly unjust society, closing their eyes to all kinds of evil and, indeed, perhaps participating in that evil, at least by default, concerned only with their own compartmentalized life of piety, closed off from everything else on the face of the earth.

—Life and Holiness

MARCH 8

A Sham Desert

A priest speaking at the funeral of Bernanos said of him: "That demand to exist authentically, that anguish at the thought that perhaps he might have only pretended to live —these marked with a devouring dissatisfaction his own estimate of himself, his view of us, his judgment of the world."

The whole thing is in this.

The real trouble with "the world," in the bad sense which

the Gospel condemns, is that it is a complete and systematic sham, and he who follows it ends not by living but by pretending he is alive, and justifying his pretense by an appeal to the general conspiracy of all others to do the same.

It is this pretense that must be vomited out in the desert. But when the monastery is only a way-station to the desert, when it remains permanently that and nothing else, then one is neither in the world nor out of it. One lives marginally, with one foot in the general sham. Too often the other foot is in a sham desert, and that is the worst of all.

—Conjectures of a Guilty Bystander

MARCH 9

A Deep Meaning

Hell is where no one has anything in common with anybody else except the fact that they all hate one another and cannot get away from one another and from themselves.

And yet the world, with all its wars, is not yet hell. And history, however terrible, has another and a deeper meaning. For it is not the evil of history that is its significance, and it is not by the evil of our time that our time can be understood. In the furnace of war and hatred, the City of those who love one another is drawn and fused together in the heroism of charity under suffering, while the city of those who hate everything is scattered and dispersed, and its citizens are cast out in every direction, like sparks, smoke, and flame.

—New Seeds of Contemplation

MARCH 10

Dull as Sin

There is nothing interesting about sin, or about evil as evil.

And the greatest sinners are the most boring people in the world, because they are also the most bored and the ones who find life most tedious.

—*New Seeds of Contemplation*

MARCH 11
Conventional Wisdom

Most men cannot live fruitfully without a large proportion of fiction in their thinking. If they do not have some efficacious mythology around which to organize their activities, they will regress into a less efficacious, more primitive, more chaotic set of illusions. When the ancients said that the solitary was likely to be either a god or a beast, they meant that he would either achieve a rare intellectual and spiritual independence or sink into a more complete and brutish dependence. The solitary easily plunges into a cavern of darkness and of phantoms more horrible and more absurd than the most inane set of conventional social images. The suffering he must then face is neither salutary nor noble. It is catastrophic.

—*Disputed Questions*

MARCH 12
Born Loser

In the eyes of our conformist society, the hermit is nothing but a failure. He has to be a failure—we have absolutely no use for him, no place for him. He is outside all our projects, plans, assemblies, movements. We can countenance him as long as he remains only a fiction, or a dream. As soon as he becomes real, we are revolted by his insignificance, his poverty, his shabbiness, his total lack of status.

—Disputed Questions

MARCH 13
No Place for Truth

How is it that our comfortable society has lost its sense of the value of truthfulness? Life has become so easy that we think we can get along without telling the truth. A liar no longer needs to feel that his lies may involve him in starvation. If living were a little more precarious, and if a person who could not be trusted found it more difficult to get along with other men, we would not deceive ourselves and one another so carelessly.

But the whole world has learned to deride veracity or to ignore it. Half the civilized world makes a living by telling lies. Advertising, propaganda, and all the other forms of publicity that have taken the place of truth have taught men to take it for granted that they can tell other people whatever they like, provided that it sounds plausible and evokes some kind of shallow emotional response.

—No Man Is an Island

MARCH 14
Dark of Mind

Last night it snowed again. The sky looks like lead. It is about as dark as my own mind. I see nothing, I understand nothing. I am sorry for complaining and making a disturbance. All I want is to please God and to do his will.

—The Sign of Jonas

MARCH 15

At Peace with Time

The Liturgy accepts our common, everyday experience of time: sunrise, noonday, sunset; spring, summer, autumn, winter. . . . The Christian does not, or at any rate need not, consider time an enemy. Time is not doing him any harm, time is not standing between him and anything he desires. Time is not robbing him of anything he treasures.

To understand the attitude of the Christian and of the Liturgy toward time, we must have a profound understanding of Christian hope and Christian trust. Fundamentally, the Christian is at peace with time because he is at peace with God. Time has now come to terms with man's freedom.

Hence the Christian is not afraid of the clock, nor is he in cunning complicity with it. The Christian life is not really a "victory over time," because time is not and cannot be a real antagonist. Of course, the Christian life is a victory over death: but it is a victory which accepts death and accepts the lapse of time that inevitably leads to death. But it does this in a full consciousness that death is in no sense a "triumph of time." For the Christian, time is no longer the devourer of all things.

—Seasons of Celebration

MARCH 16

Tyrannies of Soul

Suggested emendation in the Lord's Prayer: Take out "Thy Kingdom come" and substitute "Give us time!"
—Conjectures of a Guilty Bystander

The history of the world, with the material destruction of cities and nations and people, expressed the interior division that tyrannizes the souls of all men, and even of the saints.

—New Seeds of Contemplation

MARCH 17

A World Burning

Sooner or later the world must burn, and all things in it— all the books, the cloister together with the brothels, Fra Angelico together with the Lucky Strike ads, which I haven't seen for seven years, because I don't remember seeing one in Louisville. Sooner or later, it will all be consumed by fire and nobody will be left—for by that time the last man in the universe will have discovered the bomb capable of destroying the universe, and will have been unable to resist the temptation to throw the thing and get it over with.

And here I sit writing a diary.

But love laughs at the end of the world, because love is the door to eternity; and, before anything can happen, love will have drawn him over the sill and closed the door, and he won't bother about the world burning because he will know nothing about love.

—The Sign of Jonas

MARCH 18

Joy in Mid-Lent

My chief joy is to escape to the attic of the garden house

and the little broken window that looks out over the valley. There in the silence I love the green grass. The tortured gestures of the apple trees have become part of my prayer. I look at the shining water under the willows and listen to the sweet songs of all the living things that are in our woods and fields. So much do I love this solitude that when I walk out along the road to the old barns that stand alone, far from the new buildings, delight begins to overpower me from head to foot and peace smiles even in the marrow of my bones.

—*The Sign of Jonas*

MARCH 19

The Real World

In the midst of reciting the *Benedicite,* I saw the great presence of the sun, which had just risen behind the cedar trees. And now under the pines the sun has made a great golden basilica of fire and water.

Perspective: crows making a racket in the east, dogs making a racket in the west—yet, over all, the majestic peace of Sunday. Is this, after all, the real picture of our world?

—*Conjectures of a Guilty Bystander*

MARCH 20

Liberation and Light

Do everything you can to avoid the noise and the business of men. Keep as far away as you can from the places where they gather to cheat and insult one another, to exploit one another, to laugh at one another, or to mock one another with their false gestures of friendship. Be glad if you can keep beyond the reach of their radios. Do not bother with their unearthly songs. Do not read their advertisements.

The contemplative life certainly does not demand a self-righteous contempt for the habits and diversions of ordinary people. Nevertheless, no man who seeks liberation and light in solitude, no man who seeks spiritual freedom, can afford to yield passively to all the appeals of a society of salesmen, advertisers, and consumers. There is no doubt that life cannot be lived on a human level without certain legitimate pleasures. But to say that all the pleasures which offer themselves to us as necessities are now "legitimate" is quite another story.

—New Seeds of Contemplation

MARCH 21

True Solitude

True solitude is the home of the person, false solitude the refuge of the individualist.

—New Seeds of Contemplation

MARCH 22

Pretending a Purpose

Those who love their own noise are impatient of everything else. They constantly defile the silence of the forests and the mountains and the sea. They bore through silent nature in every direction with their machines, for fear that the calm world might accuse them of their own emptiness. The urgency of their swift movement seems to ignore the tranquility of nature by pretending to have a purpose. The loud plane seems for a moment to deny the reality of the clouds and of the sky by its direction, its noise, and its pretended strength. The silence of the sky remains when the plane has gone. The tranquility of the clouds will remain when the plane has fallen apart. It is the silence of the world that is real. Our noise, our business, and all our fatuous statements about our purposes—these are the illusions.

—No Man Is an Island

MARCH 23

Closing the Door

One of the worst illusions in the life of contemplation would be to try to find God by barricading yourself inside your own soul, shutting out all external reality by sheer concentration and will-power, cutting yourself off from the world and other men by stuffing yourself inside your own mind and closing the door like a turtle.

—New Seeds of Contemplation

MARCH 24

The Way We Are Made

It is not possible for man to live so separated from others, so isolated and private in his own heart, that his secret selfishness and sin will not affect others. We are involved in each other's lives, not by choice but by necessity, for that is the way we are made. No man can pretend successfully to live purely in his own private universe and remain sane. The very condition of normal human life is community, communication, and "conversation" in the old Latin sense of *conversatio,* exchange on the level of social living.

The lives of all men are inextricably mixed together, and

the salvation and damnation of souls is involved in this inescapable communication of freedoms. Either we will love and help one another or we will hate and attack one another, in which latter case we will all be one another's hell. Perhaps Sartre was not far wrong in saying that where freedom is abused, society itself turns into hell. ("L'enfer c'est les autres.")

—*Seasons of Celebration*

MARCH 25

Pleasing the Devil

The devils are very pleased with a soul that comes out of its dry house and shivers in the rain for no other reason than that the house is dry.

—*New Seeds of Contemplation*

MARCH 26

Rediscovering God

Now it is evening. The frogs still sing. After the showers of rain around dinner time the sky cleared. All afternoon I sat on the bed rediscovering the meaning of contemplation—rediscovering God, rediscovering myself—and the office, and Scripture and everything.

It has been one of the most wonderful days I have ever known in my life, and yet I am not attached to that part of it either. Any pleasure or the contentment I may have got out of silence and solitude and freedom from all care does not matter. But I know that is the way I ought to be living: with my mind and senses silent, contact with the world of business and war and community troubles severed—not solicitous for anything high or low or far or near. Not pushing myself around with my own fancies or desires or projects—and not letting myself get hurried off my feet by the excessive current of natural activity that flows through the universe with full force.

—*The Sign of Jonas*

A Mystery

The life of every man is a mystery of solitude and communion.

—*The Living Bread*

MARCH 27

Good Friday

I had a pious thought, but I am not going to write it down. It is raining. The best place to hide, this afternoon, was in the church. It rained hard and you could hear the rain beating all over the long roof.

I had a thought about the Psalter, too, but I will not put that down either. The thoughts that come to me are stupid.

I feel knocked out, but I can think of no good reason for wanting to feel otherwise. There is not much use in making long speeches to Jesus about our pains, especially on Good Friday.

—*The Sign of Jonas*

MARCH 28

Dark Before Dawn

If the future seems dark to us, is it not perhaps because we are witnessing the dawn of a light that has never before been seen? We live in an age in which charity can become heroic as it has never been before. We live, perhaps, on the threshold of the greatest eucharistic era of the world—the era that may well witness the final union of all mankind.

—The Living Bread

To Wait in Peace

And then to wait in peace and emptiness and oblivion of all things. *Bonum est praestolari cum silento salutare Dei.* ("It is good to wait in silence for the salvation of God.")

—New Seeds of Contemplation

MARCH 29

Easter

In the old days, on Easter night, the Russian peasants used to carry the blest fire home from church. The light would scatter and travel in all directions through the darkness, and the desolation of the night would be pierced and dispelled as lamps came on in the windows of the farmhouses one by one.

Even so, the glory of God sleeps everywhere, ready to blaze out unexpectedly in created things. Even so, his peace and his order lie hidden in the world, even the world of today, ready to reestablish themselves in his way, in his own good time: but never without the instrumentality of free options made by free men.

—The New Man

A Discovery of God

The grace of Easter is a great silence, an immense tranquility, and a clean taste in your soul. It is the taste of heaven, but not the heaven of some wild exaltation. The Easter of the soul is not riot and drunkenness of spirit, but a discovery of order—above all, order—a discovery of God and all things in him. This is a wine without intoxication, a joy that has no poison hidden in it. It is life without death.

—*The Sign of Jonas*

MARCH 30

Peace and Meaning

The less said about the Easter morning Pontifical Mass the better. Interminable pontifical maneuverings, with the "Master of Ceremonies" calling every play, and trying to marshal the ministers into formation and keep things moving. Purple zuchetto and cappa magna and, of course, it has to be our Mexican novice who was appointed to carry the long train (this inwardly made me furious and practically choked any desire I may have had to sing alleluias). The church was stifling with solemn, feudal, and unbreathable fictions. This taste for plush, for ornamentation, for display strikes me as secular, no matter how much it is supposed to be "for the glory of God."

The spring outside seemed much more sacred. Easter afternoon I went to the lake and sat in silence, looking at the green buds, the wind skimming the utterly silent surface of the water, a muskrat slowly paddling to the other side. Peace and meaning. Sweet spring air. One could breathe. The alleluias came back by themselves.

—*Conjectures of a Guilty Bystander*

Souls Like Wax

Souls are like wax waiting for a seal. By themselves they have no special identity. The wax that has melted in God's will can easily receive the stamp of its identity, the truth of what it was meant to be.

—New Seeds of Contemplation

MARCH 31

A Prayer of Glory

Justify my soul, O God, but also from your fountains fill my will with fire. Shine in my mind, though perhaps this means "be darkness to my experience," but occupy my heart with your tremendous life.

Let my eyes see nothing in the world but your glory, and let my hands touch nothing that is not for your service. Let my tongue taste no bread that does not strengthen me to praise your great mercy.

I will hear your voice and I will hear all harmonies you have created, singing your hymns.

Sheep's wool and cotton from the field shall warm me enough that I may live in your service; I will give the rest to your poor. Let me use all things for one sole reason: to find my joy in giving your glory.

Therefore, keep me, above all things, from sin. Keep me from the dead works of vanity and the thankless labor in which artists destroy themselves for pride and money and reputation, and saints are smothered under the avalanche of their own importunate zeal.

But give me the strength that waits upon you in silence and peace.

—New Seeds of Contemplation

April

APRIL 1

Innocent Speech

I came up here from the monastery last night, sloshing through the cornfield, said Vespers, and put some oatmeal on the Coleman stove for supper. It boiled over while I was listening to the rain and toasting a piece of bread at the log fire. The night became very dark. The rain surrounded the whole cabin with its enormous virginal myth, a whole world of meaning, of secrecy, of silence, of rumor. Think of it: all that speech pouring down, selling nothing, judging nobody, drenching the thick mulch of dead leaves, soaking the trees, filling the gullies and crannies of the woods with water, washing out the places where men have stripped the hillside! What a thing it is to sit absolutely alone, in the forest, at night, cherished by this wonderful, unintelligible, perfectly innocent speech, the most comforting speech in the world, the talk that rain makes by itself all over the ridges, and the talk of the watercourses everywhere in the hollows!

—*Raids on the Unspeakable*

APRIL 2

In Muted Solitude

Today I was back again by the garden house and in the mute solitude that is indifferent to verbal communication. The sun was warm and all the living creatures sang.

—*The Sign of Jonas*

APRIL 3

Worship in Secret

Let there be a place somewhere in which you can breathe naturally, quietly, and not have to take your breath in continuously short gasps. A place where your mind can be idle, and forget its concerns, descend into silence, and worship the Father in secret. There can be no contemplation where there is no secret.

—*New Seeds of Contemplation*

APRIL 4

Suffering Their Bluff

Thoreau sat in his cabin and criticized the railways. I sit in mine and wonder about a world that has—well, progressed. I must read *Walden* again, and see if Thoreau already guessed that he was part of what he thought he could escape. But it is not a matter of "escaping." It is not even a matter of protesting very audibly.

Technology is here, even in the cabin. True, the utility line is not here yet, and so G.E. is not here yet either. When the utilities and G.E. enter my cabin, arm in arm, it will be nobody's fault but my own. I admit it. I am not kidding anybody, even myself. I will suffer their bluff and patronizing complacencies in silence. I will let them think they know what I am doing here.

—*Raids on the Unspeakable*

APRIL 5

A Lucid Silence

The best thing for me is a lucid silence that does not even imagine it speaks to anybody. A silence in which I see no interlocutor, frame no message for anyone, formulate no word either for man or paper. There will still be plenty to say when the time comes to write, and what is written will be simpler and more fruitful.

—*The Sign of Jonas*

Announcement

The rain ceases, and a bird's clear song suddenly announces the difference between heaven and hell.

—*No Man Is an Island*

APRIL 6

The Present Festival

The rain has stopped. The afternoon sun slants through the pine trees, and how those useless needles smell in the clear air!

A dandelion, long out of season, has pushed itself into bloom between the smashed leaves of last summer's day lilies. The valley resounds with the totally uninformative talk of creeks and wild water.

Then the quails begin their sweet whistling in the wet bushes. Their noise is absolutely useless, and so is the delight I take in it. There is nothing I would rather hear, not because it is better noise than other noises, but because it is the voice of the present moment, the present festival.

Yet even here the earth shakes. Over Fort Knox the Rhinoceros is having fun.

—*Raids on the Unspeakable*

APRIL 7

One Good Morning

A spring morning alone in the woods. Sunrise: the enormous yoke of energy spreading and spreading as if to take over the entire sky. After that: the ceremonies of the birds feeding in the wet grass. The meadowlark, feeding and singing. Then the quiet, totally silent, dry, sun-drenched midmorning of spring, under the climbing sun.

April is not the cruelest month. Not in Kentucky. It was hard to say Psalms. Attention would get carried away in the vast blue arc of the sky, trees, hills, grass, and all things. How absolutely central is the truth that we are, first of all, part of nature, though we are a very special part, that which is conscious of God.

One has to be alone, under the sky, before everything falls into place and one finds his own place in the midst of it all. We have to have the humility to realize ourselves as part of nature. Denial of this results only in madness and cruelties. One can be part of nature, surely, without being Lady Chatterly's lover.

It was one good morning. A return in spirit to the first morning of the world.

—*Conjectures of a Guilty Bystander*

APRIL 8

A Sense of Desperation

There is a huge sense of desperation running through this whole society, with its bombs and its money and its deathwish. We are caught in the ambiguities of a colossal sense of failure in the very moment of the most phenomenal success. We have everything we ever claim to have wanted, and yet we are more dissatisfied than we have ever been.

People are eating their hearts out with fury and self-hate, just when they have all the money and all the leisure and all the opportunity, apparently, to really live. They find that the kind of life everyone dreams of is in fact impossible. They cannot face leisure. They cannot handle prosperity.

I think we would be happier in a real crisis, instead of in a constant series of imaginary ones that we cannot possibly live with. Perhaps this unconscious sense of unreality will finally drive us all into a real cataclysm, just to have the relief of getting away from fictions and imaginations!

—Conjectures of a Guilty Bystander

APRIL 9

Something Infinitely More

The desire for contemplation has nothing essential to do with art or with the aesthetic sense. It cannot be satisfied by poetry any more than it can by philosophy, or music, or ceremonies, or biblical speculations. After all, we will never come to contemplation unless we desire something infinitely more than contemplation.

—Bread in the Wilderness

APRIL 10

Lost in a Crowd

The great temptation of modern man is not physical solitude, but immersion in the mass of other men, not escape to the mountains or the desert (would that more men were so tempted!), but escape into the great formless sea of irresponsibility which is the crowd.

There is actually no more dangerous solitude than that of the man who is lost in a crowd, who does not know he is alone and who does not function as a person in the community either. He does not face the risks of true solitude or its responsibilities, and at the same time the multitude has taken all other responsibilities off his shoulders.

Yet modern man is by no means free of care; he is burdened by the diffuse, anonymous anxiety, the nameless fears, the petty itching lusts and the all-pervading hostilities which fill mass society the way water fills the ocean.

—New Seeds of Contemplation

APRIL 11

Without Anxiety

It gives great glory to God for a person to live in this world, using and appreciating the good things of life without care, without anxiety, and without inordinate passion.

—No Man Is an Island

Ordinary Life

We should not need so much austerity to learn to be content with ordinary life.

—Conjectures of a Guilty Bystander

APRIL 12

To Know Ourselves

We cannot be ourselves unless we know ourselves. But self-knowledge is impossible when thoughtless and automatic activity keeps our souls in confusion. To know ourselves, it is not necessary to cease all activity in order to think about ourselves. That would be useless, and would probably do most of us a great deal of harm. But we have to cut down our activity to the point where we can think calmly and reasonably about our actions.

We cannot begin to know ourselves until we can see the real reasons why we do the things we do, and we cannot be ourselves until our actions correspond to our intentions, and our intentions are appropriate to our own situation.

But that is enough. It is not necessary that we succeed in everything. A man can be perfect and still reap no fruit from his work, and it may happen that a man who is able to accomplish very little is much more of a person than another who seems to accomplish very much.

—No Man Is an Island

APRIL 13

Our True Face

If we take our vulnerable shell to be our true identity, if we think our mask is our true face, we will protect it with fabrications even at the cost of violating our own truth.

—*Raids on the Unspeakable*

APRIL 14

The Problem of Love

The whole problem of our time is the problem of love: how are we going to recover the ability to love ourselves and to love one another? The reason why we hate one another and fear one another is that we secretly, or openly, hate and fear our own selves. And we hate ourselves because the depths of our being are a chaos of frustration and spiritual misery. Lonely and helpless, we cannot be at peace with others because we are not at peace with ourselves, and we cannot be at peace with ourselves because we are not at peace with God.

—*The Living Bread*

APRIL 15

A Way of Knowing

The inmost self is beyond the kind of experience which says "I want," "I love," "I know," "I feel." It has its own way of knowing, loving, and experiencing, which is a divine way and not a human one, a way of identity, of union, of "espousal," in which there is no longer a separate psychological individuality drawing all good and all truth toward itself, and thus loving and knowing for itself. Lover and Beloved are "one spirit."

—New Seeds of Contemplation

APRIL 16
Blaze of Recognition

Under the pressure of a very great love, or in the darkness of a conflict that exacts a heroic renunciation of our whole self, or in the ecstasy of a sudden joy that does not belong to this earth, the soul will be raised out of itself. It will come face to face with the Christ of the Psalms.

In an experience that might be likened to a flash of dark lightning, a thunderclap over the surface of the abyss, "its eyes will be opened and it will know him and he will vanish from its sight." This momentary blaze of recognition is not produced by a created species or image in the soul.

It is the flash of a flame that is touched off by an immediate contact of the substance of the soul with God Himself. In one terrific second that belongs not to time but to eternity, the whole soul is transfixed and illumined by the tremendous darkness which is the light of God.

—Bread in the Wilderness

APRIL 17
Says My Shadow

Let us walk along here, says my shadow, and compose a number of sentences, each one of which begins: "You think you are a monk, but . . ."

—Conjectures of a Guilty Bystander

APRIL 18

Some Other Poet

Many poets are not poets for the same reason that many religious men are not saints: they never succeed in being themselves. They never get around to being the particular poet or the particular monk they are intended to be by God. They never become the man or the artist who is called for by all the circumstances of their individual lives.

They waste their years in vain efforts to be some other poet, some other saint. For many absurd reasons, they are convinced that they are obliged to become somebody else who died two hundred years ago and who lived in circumstances utterly alien to their own.

They wear out their minds and bodies in a hopeless endeavor to have somebody else's experiences or write somebody else's poems or possess somebody else's spirituality.

Hurry ruins saints as well as artists. They want quick success, and they are in such haste to get it that they cannot take time to be true to themselves. And when the madness is upon them they argue that their very haste is a species of integrity.

—New Seeds of Contemplation

APRIL 19

A False Self

Every one of us is shadowed by an illusory person: a false self.

—New Seeds of Contemplation

APRIL 20

Between Silence and Silence

Words stand between silence and silence: between the silence of things and the silence of our own being. Between the silence of the world and the silence of God. When we have really met and known the world in silence, words do not separate us from the world nor from other men, nor from God, nor from ourselves, because we no longer trust entirely in language to contain reality.

Truth rises from the silence of being to the quiet, tremendous presence of the Word. Then, sinking again into silence, the truth of words bears us down into the silence of God. Or rather God rises out of the sea like a treasure in the waves, and when language recedes his brightness remains on the shores of our own being.

—Thoughts in Solitude

APRIL 21

At Least One Room

There should be at least one room, or some corner, where no one will find you and disturb you or notice you. You should be able to untether yourself from the world and set yourself free, loosing all the fine strings and strands of tension that bind you, by sight, by sound, by thought, to the presence of other men.

—New Seeds of Contemplation

APRIL 22

Prayer As Inner Upheaval

All good meditative prayer is a conversion of our entire self to God. One cannot, then, enter into meditation, in this sense, without a kind of inner upheaval. By upheaval I do not mean a disturbance, but a breaking out of routine, a liberation of the heart from the cares and preoccupations of one's daily business.

The reason why so few people apply themselves seriously to mental prayer is precisely that this inner upheaval is necessary, and they are usually incapable of the effort required to make it. It may be that they lack generosity, and it may also be that they lack direction and experience, and go about it the wrong way.

They disturb themselves, they throw themselves into agitation by the violent efforts they make to get recollected, and finally they end in hopelessness. They compromise, in the end, by a series of frustrated routines which help them to pass the time, or else they relax into a state of semi-coma which, they hope, can be justified by the name of contemplation.

—Thoughts in Solitude

Too Much Happening

No matter how empty our lives become, we are always at least convinced that something is happening because, indeed, as we so often complain, too much is happening.

—Conjectures of a Guilty Bystander

APRIL 23

Spiritual Servitude

We live in a climate of individualism. But our individualism is in decay. Our tradition of freedom, which, as a matter of fact, is rooted in a deeply Christian soil, and which in itself is worthy of the highest respect and loyalty, has begun to lose its genuine vitality. It is becoming more and more a verbal convention rather than a spiritual conviction.

The tendency to substitute words about freedom for the reality of freedom itself has brought us to a state of ambivalent spiritual servitude. The noise with which we protest our love of freedom tends to be proportionate to our actual fear of genuine freedom, and our guilt of our unconscious refusal to pay the price of freedom. The agitated and querulous license with which we abandon ourselves to our own fantasies is a purely subjective and fallacious excuse for freedom.

—Seasons of Celebration

APRIL 24

A Lost Capacity

The question arises: is modern man—confused and exhausted by a multitude of words, opinions, doctrines, and slogans—psychologically capable of the clarity and confidence necessary for valid prayer? Is he not so frustrated and deafened by conflicting propagandas that he has lost his capacity for deep and simple trust?

—Life and Holiness

APRIL 25

The Great Way

Zen story:
A monk said to Joshu: "What is the way?"
Joshu replied: "Outside the fence."
The monk insisted: "I mean the Great Way? What is the Great Way?"
Joshu replied: "The Great Way is that which leads to the Capital."

The Great Way is right in the middle of the story, and I should remember it when I get excited about war and peace. I sometimes think I have an urgent duty to make all kinds of protest and clarification—but, above all, the important thing is to be on the Great Way and stay on it, whether one speaks or not. It is not necessary to run all over the countryside shouting "peace, peace!" But it is essential to stay on the Great Way which leads to the Capital, for only on the Great Way is there peace. If no one follows the way, there will be no peace in the world, no matter how much men may preach it.

It is easy to know that "there is a way somewhere," and even perhaps to know that others are not on it (by analogy with one's own lostness, wandering far from the way). But this knowledge is useless unless it helps one find the way.

—Conjectures of a Guilty Bystander

APRIL 26

Meister Eckhart

Meister Eckhart may have limitations, but I am entranced with him nevertheless. I like the brevity, the incisiveness of his sermons, his way of piercing straight to the heart of the inner life, the awakened spark, the creative and redeeming Word, God born in us. He is a great man who was pulled down by a lot of little men who thought they could destroy him, who thought they could drag him to Avignon and have him utterly discredited. And indeed he was ruined, after his death, in twenty-eight propositions which might doubtless be found somewhere in him, but which had none of his joy, his energy, his freedom. They were not "his" in the sense that they were not at all what he intended. But they could be made to coincide with words that he had spoken. And I suppose one must take such things into account. Eckhart did not have the kind of mind that wasted time being cautious about every comma: he trusted men to recognize that what he saw was worth seeing because it brought obvious fruits of life and joy. For him, that was what mattered. But the little men had other things in mind.

—Conjectures of a Guilty Bystander

APRIL 27

A New Center

Yesterday and the day before, I felt as if I had found a new center. Something I could not grasp or understand: but nothing else in the world seemed worth trying to grasp or understand either. So I grasp nothing and understand nothing and am immensely happy.

—The Sign of Jonas

APRIL 28

Everything Holy

Everything healthy, everything certain, everything holy: if we can find such things, they all need to be emphasized and articulated. For this it is necessary that there be a genuine and deep communication between the hearts and minds of men, communication and not the noise of slogans or the repetition of clichés. Genuine communication is becoming more and more difficult, and when speech is in danger of perishing or being perverted in the amplified noise of beasts, perhaps it becomes obligatory for a monk to try to speak. There is, therefore, it seems to me, every reason why we should attempt to cry out to one another and comfort one another, insofar as this may be possible, with the truth of Christ and also with the truth of humanism and reason.

—Seeds of Destruction

APRIL 29

At Every Moment

That which is oldest is most new. The "latest" is always stillborn. It never even manages to arrive. What is really new is what was there all the time. The really new is that which at every moment, springs freshly into new existence.

—New Seeds of Contemplation

Consecrated to God

The special clumsy beauty of the particular colt on this April day in this field under these clouds is a holiness consecrated to God by his own creative wisdom, and it declares the glory of God.

The pale flowers of the dogwood outside this window are saints. The little yellow flowers that nobody notices on the edge of that road are saints looking up into the face of God. This leaf has its own texture and its own pattern of veins and its own holy shape, and the bass and trout hiding in the deep pools of the river are canonized by their beauty and their strength.

The lakes hidden among the hills are saints, and the sea is a saint who praises God without interruption in her majestic dance.

The great, gashed, half-naked mountain is another of God's natural saints. There is no other like him. He is alone in his own character; nothing else in the world ever did, or ever will, imitate God in quite the same way. That is his sanctity.

—*New Seeds of Contemplation*

APRIL 30

Loved and Praised

Let this be my only consolation: that, wherever I am, you, my Lord, are loved and praised.

The trees, indeed, love you without knowing you. The tiger lilies and corn flowers are there, proclaiming that they love you, without being aware of your presence. The beautiful dark clouds ride slowly across the sky, musing on you, like children who do not know what they are dreaming of, as they play.

But in the midst of them all, I know you, and I know of your presence. In them and in me I know of the love which they do not know, and, what is greater, I am abashed by the presence of your love in me.

O kind and terrible love, which you have given me, and which could never be in my heart if you did not love me! For in the midst of these beings which have never offended you, I am loved by you; and, it would seem, most of all, as one who has offended you. I am seen by you under the sky, and my offenses have been forgotten by you—but I have not forgotten them.

—*Thoughts in Solitude*

May

MAY 1

Praise Him

The frogs have begun singing their pleasure in all the waters and in the warm green places where the sunshine is wonderful. Praise Christ, all you living creatures. For him, you and I were created. With every breath we love him. My psalms fulfill your dim, unconscious song, O brothers in this wood.

—*The Sign of Jonas*

MAY 2

After May Day, What?

Collective life is often organized on the basis of cunning, doubt, and guilt. True solidarity is destroyed by the political art of pitting one man against another and by the commercial art of estimating all men at a price. On these illusory measurements men build a world of arbitrary values without life and meaning, full of sterile agitation. To set one man against another, one life against another, one work against another, and to express the measurement in terms of cost or of economic privilege and moral honor is to infect everybody with the deepest metaphysical doubt.

Divided and set up against one another for the purpose of evaluation, men immediately acquire the mentality of objects for sale in a slave market. They despair of themselves because they know they have been unfaithful to life and to being, and they no longer find anyone to forgive the infidelity.

—*Raids on the Unspeakable*

May 3

Cycle of Salvation

For fallen and unredeemed man, the cycle of seasons, the wheel of time itself, is only a spiritual prison. Each new spring brings a temporary hope. Autumn and winter destroy that hope with their ever-returning reminder of death.

For man in Christ, the cycle of the seasons is something entirely new: it has become a cycle of salvation. The year is not just another year: it is the year of the Lord—a year in which the passage of time itself brings us not only the natural renewal of spring and the fruitfulness of an earthly summer, but also the spiritual and interior fruitfulness of grace.

—Seasons of Celebration

May 4

Grace and Good Desires

Our liberation, our solitude, our vision, our understanding and our salvation do not depend on anything remote from us or beyond our reach. Grace has been given us along with our good desires. What is needed is the faith to accept it and the energy to put our faith to work in situations that may not seem to us to be promising. The Holy Spirit will do the rest.

—Contemplation in a World of Action

Liberation of Mind

What is important is not liberation from the body, but

liberation from the mind. We are not entangled in our own
body, but entangled in our own mind.

—*The Asian Journal of Thomas Merton*

MAY 5

Innocence and Solidarity

All innocence is a matter of belief. I do not speak now of
organized agreement, but of interior personal convictions
"in the spirit." These convictions are as strong and undeni-
able as life itself. They are rooted in fidelity to life rather
than to artificial systems. The solidarity of poets is an elemental fact like sunlight, like the seasons, like the rain. It is
something that cannot be organized, it can only happen. It
can only be "received." It is a gift to which we must remain
open. No man can plan to make the sun rise or the rain fall.
The sea is still wet despite all formal and abstract programs.
Solidarity is not collectivity. The organizers of collective life
will deride the seriousness or the reality of our hope. If they
infect us with their doubt, we shall lose our innocence and
our solidarity along with it.

—*Raids on the Unspeakable*

MAY 6

Uncertainty

Because modern man is in a state of uncertainty, we must
not be too quick to think that what he wants is absolute
certainty at any price.

—*Contemplation in a World of Action*

The Freedom of Orthodoxy

The fear of placing rules, thoughts, and words above the fact or outside the fact, this fear is important in Orthodoxy, is the basis of the freedom of the Orthodox.

—*Woods, Shore, Desert*

MAY 7

Innocent Bystander

You can easily guess that in using the term "innocent bystander" I had to examine my conscience to see whether I was being facetious. I do not remember if I smiled when I first thought of it; but, in any case, I am no longer smiling. For I do not think the question of our innocence can be a matter for jesting, and I am no longer certain that it is honorable to stand by as the helpless witness to a cataclysm, with no other hope than to die innocently and by accident, as a nonparticipant.

—*Raids on the Unspeakable*

MAY 8

Our Own Mistakes

It is when we are angry at our own mistakes that we tend most of all to deny ourselves for love of ourselves. We want to shake off the hateful thing that has humbled us. In our rush to escape the humiliation of our own mistakes, we run head-first into the opposite error—seeking comfort and compensation. And so we spend our lives running back and forth from one attachment to another.

—The Sign of Jonas

Unlike Anyone Else

Humility consists in being precisely the person you actually are before God; and since no two people are alike, if you have the humility to be yourself, you will not be like anyone else in the whole universe.

—New Seeds of Contemplation

MAY 9

Avoiding Extremes

There are two extremes to be avoided. On the one hand, there is the error of those who believe that creation is evil and who therefore seek salvation and sanctity in an exaggerated asceticism that tries to sever the soul entirely from the rest of creation. This is the spiritual disease called "angelism." On the other hand, there is the error of those who act as if divine charity made no practical demands on human conduct: as if grace were merely a quality injected into our natural lives, making them automatically pleasing and meritorious in the sight of God, without any obligation on our part to live on the supernatural level of faith and Christian virtue. This attitude sometimes usurps the name of "humanism."

—Seasons of Celebration

MAY 10

Praise and Blame

If you call one thing vile and another precious, if you praise success and blame failure, you will fill the world with thieves, soldiers, and businessmen. I have praised the saints and I have told at what cost they strove to surpass lesser men. What madness have I not preached in sermons!

—*Conjectures of a Guilty Bystander*

MAY 11

True Communication

Where men live huddled together without true communication, there seems to be greater sharing and a more genuine communion. But this is not communion, only immersion in the general meaninglessness of countless slogans and clichés repeated over and over again so that in the end one listens without hearing and responds without thinking. The constant din of empty words and machine noises, the endless booming of loudspeakers end by making true communication and true communion almost impossible.

Each individual in the mass is insulated by thick layers of insensibility. He doesn't care, he doesn't hear, he doesn't think. He does not act, he is pushed. He does not talk, he produces conventional sounds when stimulated by the appropriate noises. He does not think, he secretes clichés.

—*New Seeds of Contemplation*

May 12

Air-Conditioned Nightmare

Even where war has not yet touched them, cities are in devastation and nonentity: and yet, once again, under the surface of glitter and trash, in the midst of all the mess of traffic, there are the people, sick and distraught, drunk, mad, melancholy, anguished, or simply bored to extinction. It is the people that I love, not their roles in the city and not the glitter of business and of progress. Can't we do something more than give them air-conditioning?

—*Conjectures of a Guilty Bystander*

May 13

If You Live in a City

If you have to live in a city and work among machines and ride in the subways and eat in a place where the radio makes you deaf with spurious news, and where the food destroys your life and the sentiments of those around you poison your heart with boredom, do not be impatient, but accept it as the love of God and as a seed of solitude planted in your soul.

If you are appalled by those things, you will keep your appetite for the healing silence of recollection. Meanwhile, keep your sense of compassion for the men who have forgotten the very concept of solitude. You, at least, know that it exists, and that it is the source of peace and joy. You can still hope for such joy. They do not even hope for it anymore.

—*New Seeds of Contemplation*

MAY 14

The Inhabitants

The city itself lives on its own myth. Instead of waking up and silently existing, the city people prefer a stubborn and fabricated dream; they do not care to be a part of the night, or to be merely of the world. They have constructed a world outside the world, against the world, a world of mechanical fictions which condemn nature and seek only to use it up, thus preventing it from renewing itself and man.

—Raids on the Unspeakable

MAY 15

Caves of Silence

City churches are sometimes quiet and peaceful solitudes, caves of silence, where a man can seek refuge from the intolerable arrogance of the business world. One can be more alone, sometimes, in church than in a room in one's own house. At home, one can always be routed out and disturbed (and one should not resent this, for love sometimes demands it). But in these quiet churches one remains nameless, undisturbed in the shadows, where there are only a few chance, anonymous strangers among the vigil lights, and the curious impersonal postures of the bad statues. The very tastelessness and shabbiness of some churches makes them greater solitudes, though churches should not be vulgar. Even so, as long as they are dark, it makes little difference.

—New Seeds of Contemplation

MAY 16

The Single Quest

An individualistic quest of "contemplation" has often resulted in fanciful regression to a tepid womb of oceanic feelings.

—*Contemplation in a World of Action*

No Real Significance

The sins of art and of religion in our Western culture have been so great! Someone has to acknowledge them. I have no interest either in pop art or in religionless religion, and I think neither has any real significance for man. In ten years the whole scene will have changed, and they will be forgotten.

—*Conjectures of a Guilty Bystander*

MAY 17

False Images

I am certainly no judge of television, since I have never watched it. All I know is that there is a sufficiently general agreement, among men whose judgment I respect, that commercial television is degraded, meretricious, and absurd. Certainly, it would seem that TV could become a kind of unnatural surrogate for contemplation: a completely inert subjection to vulgar images, a descent to a subnatural passivity rather than an ascent to a supremely active passivity in understanding and love. It would seem that television should be used with extreme care and discrimination by anyone who might hope to take interior life seriously.

—New Seeds of Contemplation

MAY 18

A Concept of Sanity

And so I ask myself: what is the meaning of a concept of sanity that excludes love, considers it irrelevant, and destroys our capacity to love other human beings, to respond to their needs and their sufferings, to recognize them also as persons, to apprehend their pain as one's own? Evidently, this is not necessary for "sanity" at all. It is a religious notion, a spiritual notion, a Christian notion. What business have we to equate "sanity" with "Christianity?" None at all, obviously.

—Raids on the Unspeakable

MAY 19

A Self-Centered Life

Man is not made in such a way that he can live happily without love. If his life is centered on himself, he may indeed be able to function, but in order to do so his existence is necessarily complicated by his machinery for imposing his will on others. One cannot live a self-centered life simply. Too much cheating is involved—even if one only cheats himself.

—Contemplation in a World of Action

MAY 20

The Sane Ones

It is the sane ones, the well-adapted ones, who can without qualms and without nausea aim the missiles and press the buttons that will initiate the great festival of destruction that they, the same ones, have prepared. What makes us so sure, after all, that the danger comes from a psychotic getting into a position to fire the first shot in a nuclear war? Psychotics will be suspect. The sane ones will keep them far from the button. No one suspects the sane, and the sane ones will have perfectly good reasons, logical, well-adjusted reasons, for firing the shot. They will be obeying sane orders that have come sanely down the chain of command. And because of their sanity, they will have no qualms at all. When the missiles take off, then, it will be no mistake.

—*Raids on the Unspeakable*

MAY 21

Illusions of Power

There are many acceptable and "sane" ways of indulging one's illusory claim to divine power. One can be, for example, a proud and tyrannical parent—or a tearful and demanding martyr-parent. One can be a sadistic and overbearing boss, or a nagging perfectionist. One can be a clown, or a daredevil, or a libertine. One can be rigidly conventional, or blatantly unconventional; one can be a hermit or a demagogue.

Some satisfy their desire for divinity by knowing everybody else's business; others by judging their neighbor, or telling him what to do. One can even, alas, seek sanctity and religious perfection as an unconscious satisfaction of that deep and hidden impurity of soul which is man's pride.

—*The Silent Life*

MAY 22
The Faustian Complex

There is nothing more tragic in the modern world than the misuse of power and action to which men are driven by their own Faustian misunderstandings and misapprehensions. We have more power at our disposal today than we have ever had, and yet we are more alienated and estranged from the inner ground of meaning and of love than we have ever been.

—*Contemplation in a World of Action*

MAY 23
Mercy and Magic

Mercy breaks into the world of magic and justice and overturns its apparent consistency. Mercy is inconsistent. It is therefore comic. It liberates us from the tragic seriousness of the obsessive world which we have "made up" for ourselves by yielding to our obsessions. Only mercy can liberate us from the madness of our determination to be consistent.

—*Raids on the Unspeakable*

MAY 24
Between You and Me

I have what you have not. I am what you are not. I have taken what you have failed to take and I have seized what you could never get. Therefore, you suffer and I am happy, you are despised and I am praised, you die and I live; you are nothing and I am something because you are nothing.

And thus I spend my life admiring the distance between you and me; at times, this even helps me to forget the other men who have what I have not and who have taken what I was too slow to take and who have seized what was beyond my reach, who are praised as I cannot be praised, and who live on my death.

—New Seeds of Contemplation

MAY 25
The Only Innocent One

You will perhaps find that my thought has taken on a sentimental tinge. But since the times have become what they have become, I dare to blurt this out.

Have you and I forgotten that our vocation, as innocent bystanders—and the very condition of our terrible innocence—is to do what the child did, and keep on saying the king is naked, at the cost of being condemned criminals?

Remember, the child in the tale was the only innocent one: and because of his innocence the fault of the others was kept from being criminal, and was nothing worse than foolishness. If the child had not been there, they would all have been madmen, or criminals. It was the child's cry that saved them.

—Raids on the Unspeakable

MAY 26

Living in Ash Cans

I have very little idea of what is going on in the world, but occasionally I happen to see some of the things they are writing and drawing there, and it gives me the conviction that they are all living in ash cans. It makes me glad I cannot hear what they are singing.

—*New Seeds of Contemplation*

Time to Settle

Not to run from one thought to the next, says Theophane the Recluse, but to give each one time to settle in the heart.

—*Woods, Shore, Desert*

MAY 27

Burden of Humility

Teach me to bear a humility which shows me, without ceasing, that I am a liar and a fraud and that, even though this is so, I have an obligation to strive after truth, to be as true as I can, even though I will inevitably find all my truth half poisoned with deceit.

This is the terrible thing about humility: that it is never fully successful. If it were only possible to be completely humble on this earth. But, no, that is the trouble.

You, Lord, were humble. But our humility consists in being proud and knowing all about it, and being crushed by the unbearable weight of it, and to be able to do so little about it. What man can bear to fall into such darkness?

—*Thoughts in Solitude*

MAY 28

An Unresolved Problem

The sun is rising. All the green trees are full of birds, and their song comes up out of the wet bowers of the orchard. Crows swear pleasantly in the distance, and in the depths of my soul sits God; and between him, in the depths, and the thoughts on the surface, is the veil of an unresolved problem. This problem is my own personality—in which I do not intend at any time to take an unhealthy interest.

—*The Sign of Jonas*

Cry of a Lamb

I am on the Pacific Shore—perhaps fifty miles south of Cape Mendocino. Wide open, deserted hillside frequented only by sheep and swallows, sun and wind. No people for miles either way. Breakers on the black sand. Crying gulls fly down and land neatly on their own shadows. . . . Faint cry of a lamb on the mountainside muffled by sea wind.

—*Woods, Shore, Desert*

MAY 29

The Greatest Freedom

In humility is the greatest freedom. As long as you have to defend the imaginary self that you think is important, you lose your peace of heart. As soon as you compare that shadow with the shadows of other people, you lose all joy, because you have begun to trade in unrealities, and there is no joy in things that do not exist.

As soon as you begin to take yourself seriously and imagine that your virtues are important because they are yours, you become the prisoner of your own vanity, and even your best works will blind and deceive you. Then, in order to defend yourself, you will begin to see sins and faults everywhere in the actions of other men. And the more unreasonable importance you attach to yourself and to your works, the more you will tend to build up your own idea of yourself by condemning other people.

Sometimes virtuous men are also bitter and unhappy, because they have unconsciously come to believe that all their happiness depends on their being more virtuous than others.

—New Seeds of Contemplation

A World Without Humility

If there were no humility in the world, everybody would long ago have committed suicide.

—New Seeds of Contemplation

MAY 30

Vocation to Solitude

To deliver oneself up, to hand oneself over, entrust oneself completely to the silence of a wide landscape of woods and hills, or sea, or desert; to sit still while the sun comes up over that land and fills its silences with light. To pray and work in the morning and to labor and rest in the afternoon, and to sit still again in meditation in the evening, when night falls upon that land and when the silence fills itself with darkness and with stars.

This is a true and special vocation. There are few who are willing to belong completely to such silence, to let it soak into their bones, to breathe nothing but silence, to feed on silence, and to turn the very substance of their life into a living and vigilant silence.

—Thoughts in Solitude

Water and Light

When warmth comes again to the sea, the Tritons of spring shall wake. Life shall wake underground and undersea. The fields will laugh, the woods will be drunk with flowers of rebellion, the night will make every fool sing in his sleep, and the morning will make him stand up in the sun and cover himself with water and with light.

—Raids on the Unspeakable

MAY 31

This Precious Poverty

Evening, rain, silence, joy. I believe that, where the Lord sees that small point of poverty, extenuation, and helplessness which is the heart of a monk after very long and very dry celebrations in choir, when he sees the point of indigence to which this one is reduced, he himself cannot refuse to enter this anguish, to take flesh in it, so to speak, making it instantly a small seed of infinite joy and peace and solitude in the world.

There is for me no sense, no truth in anything that elaborately contrives to hide this precious poverty, this seed of tears, which is also the seed of true joy. Demonstrations and distractions that try to take one away from this are futile. They can become infidelities if they are eagerly sought.

I may speak to others only insofar as I address myself to this same small spark of truth and sorrow in them, to help resolve their doubts, to assuage their anguish, to lighten their grief by helping them to be strong in this same small spark of exhaustion in which the Lord becomes their wisdom and their life forever.

—*Conjectures of a Guilty Bystander*

June

JUNE 1

No Other Place

It is June. Once again the cloister is paved with flowers, the sanctuary white hot under the floodlights concealed behind the pillars, high in the ceiling. You look up at the monstrance through a cloud of hot, sweet smoke from the censer, and the sweat runs down into your eyes!

I feel as though I had never been anywhere in the world except Gethsemani—as if there were no other place in the world where I had ever really lived. I do not say I love Gethsemani despite the heat, or because of the heat.

I love Gethsemani: that means burning days and nights in summer, with the sun beating down on the metal roof and the psalms pulsing exultantly through the airless choir, while, row upon row of us, a hundred and forty singers, we sway forward and bow down. And the clouds of smoke go up to God in the sanctuary, and the novices get thin and go home forever.

—The Sign of Jonas

JUNE 2

A Consuming Fire

God is a consuming Fire. He alone can refine us like gold, and separate us from the slag and dross of our selfish individualities to fuse us into this wholeness of perfect unity that will reflect his own Triune life forever.

—New Seeds of Contemplation

JUNE 3

Next to a Window

The heat has got us, and we change our torn shirts and hang them out in the sun for the sweat to dry out of them, and we sleep in work blouses. Since the floor was painted I ended up with a cell next to a window.

God talks in the trees. There is a wind, so that it is cool to sit outside. This morning at four o'clock in the clean dawn sky there were some special clouds in the west over the woods, with a very perfect and delicate pink, against deep blue. A hawk was wheeling over the trees.

Every minute life begins all over again. Amen.

—*The Sign of Jonas*

JUNE 4

The Mercy of Things

There is a mercy of individual things that spring into being without reason. They are virtuous in the sight of God because their names do not identify them. Every plant that stands in the light of the sun is a saint and an outlaw. Every tree that brings forth blossoms without the command of man is powerful in the sight of God. Every star that man has not counted is a world of sanity and perfection. Every blade of grass is an angel singing in a shower of glory.

—*Raids on the Unspeakable*

JUNE 5

Moveable Feasts

Another sunny birthday. I am tormented by poetry and

loss. The summer morning approaches with shy, tentative mandibles. There are perhaps better solutions than to be delicately eaten by an entirely favorable day. But the day is bright with love and with riches for the unconcerned.

A black butterfly dances on the blond light of hot cement. My loneliness is nourished by the smell of freshly cut grass and the distant complaint of a freight train. Nine even strokes of the bell fall like a slowly counted fortune into the far end of my mind, while I walk out at the other end of awareness into a very new hot morning in which all the symbols have to be moved.

Here is another smiling Jewish New Year, and the myths are about to be changed. We will start up brand new religious engines in the multiple temples. Tonight the dark will come alive with fireworks, and age will have scored another minor festival.

—Cables to the Ace

JUNE 6

Ordinary Possibilities

Poetry is the flowering of ordinary possibilities. It is the fruit of ordinary and natural choice. This is its innocence and dignity.

—Raids on the Unspeakable

JUNE 7

A Poet's Life

A poet spends his life in repeated projects, over and over again, attempting to build or to dream the world in which he lives. But more and more he realizes that this world is at once his and everybody's. It cannot be purely private any more than it can be purely public. It cannot be fully communicated. It grows out of a common participation which is nevertheless recorded in authentically personal images. I have without scruple mixed what is my own experience with what is almost everybody else's.

—*The Geography of Lograire*

JUNE 8

Measure of Our Being

The measure of our being is not to be sought in the violence of our experiences. Turbulence of spirit is a sign of spiritual weakness. When delights spring out of our depths like leopards, we have nothing to be proud of: our soul's life is in danger. For when we are strong we are always much greater than the things that happen to us, and the soul of a man who has found himself is like a deep sea in which there may be many fish; but they never come up out of the sea, and no one of them is big enough to trouble its placid surface. A man's "being" is far greater than anything he feels or does.

—*No Man Is an Island*

JUNE 9

Way of Authenticity

Where there is a genuine life of solitude, poverty, prayer, silence, penance, work, charity, obedience; where the Law of the Gospel, which is a law of life and grace, fully and fervently kept and not obscured by legalism and sermonizing, it will be easy to see that here is a way of authenticity and truth in which man does not merely discover and assert a private identity, a "personality" in the sense of a successful role, but learns that the truest way to find himself is to lose the self he has found in Christ.

—*Contemplation in a World of Action*

JUNE 10

Success and Failure

My successes are not my own. The way to them was prepared by others. The fruit of my labors is not my own, for I am preparing the way for the achievements of another. Nor are my failures my own. They may spring from the failure of another, but they are also compensated for by another's achievement. Therefore, the meaning of my life is not to be looked for merely in the sum total of my own achievements. It is seen only in the complete integration of my achievements and failures with the achievements and failures of my own generation, my own society and time.

—*No Man Is an Island*

JUNE 11

The Clarity of Love

Love is not mere emotion or sentiment. It is the lucid and ardent response of the whole man to a value that is revealed to him as perfect, appropriate, and urgent in the providential context of his own life. Hence, there are innumerable ways in which men can be awakened from the sleep of a mechanical existence and summoned to give himself totally in the clarity of love.

—*Contemplation in a World of Action*

JUNE 12

Saint John of the Cross

Saint John of the Cross compares man to a window through which the light of God is shining. If the window-pane is clean of every stain, it is completely transparent, we do not see it at all: it is "empty" and nothing is seen by the light.

But if a man bears in himself the stains of spiritual egotism and preoccupation with his illusory and exterior self, even in "good things," then the windowpane itself is clearly seen by reason of the stains that are on it. Hence, if a man can be rid of the stains and dust produced within him by his fixation upon what is good and bad in reference to himself, he will be transformed in God and will be "one with God."

—Zen and the Birds of Appetite

JUNE 13

Desert of Loneliness

It is in the desert of loneliness and emptiness that the fear of death and the need for self-affirmation are seen to be illusory. When this is faced, then anguish is not necessarily overcome, but it can be accepted and understood. Thus, in the heart of anguish, are found the gifts of peace and understanding: not simply in personal illumination and liberation, but by commitment and empathy, for the contemplative must assume the universal anguish and the inescapable condition of mortal man. The solitary, far from enclosing himself in himself, becomes every man. He dwells in the solitude, the poverty, the indigence of every man.

—Raids on the Unspeakable

JUNE 14

An Enemy of Candor

Fear is perhaps the greatest enemy of candor. How many men fear to follow their consciences because they would rather conform to the opinion of other men than to the truth they know in their souls. How can I be sincere if I am constantly changing my mind to conform with the shadow of what I think others expect of me? Others have no right to demand that I be anything other than what I ought to be in the sight of God.

—*No Man Is an Island*

JUNE 15

A New Light

I saw the country in a light that we usually do not see: the low-slanting rays picked out the foliage of the trees and high-lighted a new wheatfield against the dark curtain of woods on the knobs, which were in shadow.

It was very beautiful. Deep peace. Sheep on the slopes behind the sheep barn. The new trellises in the novitiate garden leaning and sagging under a hill of roses. A cardinal singing suddenly in the walnut tree, and piles of fragrant logs all around the woodshed waiting to be cut in bad weather.

I looked at all this in great tranquility, with my soul and spirit quiet. For me, landscape seems to be important for contemplation. Anyway, I have no scruples about loving it. Didn't Saint John of the Cross hide himself in a room up in a church tower, where there was one small window through which he could look out at the country?

—*The Sign of Jonas*

JUNE 16

Like a Word

God utters me like a word containing a partial thought of himself.

—*New Seeds of Contemplation*

JUNE 17

Aesthetic Experience

In an aesthetic experience, in the creation or the contemplation of a work of art, the psychological conscience is able to attain some of its highest and most perfect fulfillments. Art enables us to find ourselves and lose ourselves at the same time.

The mind that responds to the intellectual and spiritual values that lie hidden in a poem, a painting, or a piece of music, discovers a spiritual vitality that lifts it above itself, takes it out of itself, and makes it present to itself on a level of being that it did not know it could ever achieve.

—*No Man Is an Island*

JUNE 18

For Whom You Write

If you write for God, you will reach many men and bring them joy.

If you write for men, you may make some money and you

may give someone a little joy, and you may make a noise in the world—for a little while.

If you write only for yourself, you can read what you yourself have written, and after ten minutes you will be so disgusted you will wish that you were dead.

—*New Seeds of Contemplation*

JUNE 19

Music of Silence

Music is pleasing not only because of the sound but because of the silence that is in it: without the alternation of sound and silence, there would be no rhythm. If we strive to be happy by filling all the silences of life with sound, productive by turning all life's leisure into work, and real by turning all our being into doing, we will only succeed in producing a hell on earth.

If we have no silence, God is not heard in our music. If we have no rest, God does not bless our work. If we twist our lives out of shape in order to fill every corner of them with action and experience, God will silently withdraw from our hearts and leave us empty.

—*No Man Is an Island*

JUNE 20

Self-Fulfilling Prophecy

For the poet there is precisely no magic. There is only life in all its unpredictability and all its freedom. All magic is a ruthless venture in manipulation, a vicious circle, a self-fulfilling prophecy.

—*Raids on the Unspeakable*

Something Deep

Individuality does not necessarily assert itself on the surface of everyday life. It will not be a matter of mere appearances, or opinions, or tastes, or ways of doing things. It is something deep in the soul.

—New Seeds of Contemplation

JUNE 21

A New Summer

Wind and sun. Catbird bickering in a bush. Ringing bells and blowing whistles, and then squawking in a lamentable fashion. Trees are all clothed and benches are out, and a new summer has begun.

—The Sign of Jonas

JUNE 22

Joys of Silence

The world of men has forgotten the joys of silence, the peace of solitude which is necessary, to some extent, for the fullness of human living.

If man is constantly exiled from his own home, locked out of his own spiritual solitude, he ceases to be a true person. He no longer lives as a man. He is not even a healthy animal. Man becomes a kind of automaton, living without joy, because he has lost all spontaneity. He is no longer moved from within, but only from outside himself. He no longer makes decisions for himself, but lets them be made for him.

Such a man no longer acts upon the outside world, but lets it act upon him. He is propelled through life by a series of collisions with outside forces. His is no longer the life of a human being, but the existence of a sentient billiard ball, a being without a purpose and without any deeply valid response to reality.

—The Silent Life

JUNE 23

A Sense of Loss

The flowing of events: our youngest postulant, from Canada, is busy today with a wrecking bar, smashing up the partitions of the room in the old guesthouse, on the third floor, where, twenty years ago, I first came on retreat, that silent, moonlit night at the end of Lent.

I remember the spiritual awe of that night! And now, in the clear light of a summer day, the plaster crashes to the floor and sunlit clouds of dust float out the window where I wrote that poem about the abbey and Matins.

This kid was not even born then. He is the son of an airman who married an English girl, as my brother did, during the War. He was born in the Blitz, in England. And now he is tearing down that room and my own history—a fact which I gladly accept, but with this sense of loss nevertheless.

—Conjectures of a Guilty Bystander

JUNE 24

In Other Times

What was once real in other times and places becomes

real in us today. And its reality is not an official parade of externals. It is a living spirit marked by freedom and by a certain originality.

—Contemplation in a World of Action

JUNE 25

Like a River

God's love is like a river springing up in the Divine Substance and flowing endlessly through his creation, filling all things with life and goodness and strength.

—New Seeds of Contemplation

JUNE 26

The Heraclitean River

In the Republic of Plato there was already no place for poets and musicians, still less for dervishes and monks. As for the technological Platos who think they now run the world we live in, they imagine they can tempt us with banalities and abstractions. But we can elude them merely by stepping into the Heraclitean river, which is never crossed twice.

When the poet puts his foot in that ever-moving river, poetry itself is born out of the flashing water. In that unique instant, the truth is manifest to all who are able to receive it.

No one can come near the river unless he walks on his own feet. He cannot come there carried in a vehicle.

No one can enter the river wearing the garments of public and collective ideas. He must feel the water on his skin. He must know that immediacy is for naked minds only, and for the innocent.

Come, dervishes: here is the water of life. Dance in it.

—Raids on the Unspeakable

JUNE 27

Dance of Life

You fool, it is life that makes you dance: have you forgotten? The fire of a wild white sun has eaten up the distance between hope and despair. Dance in the sun, you tepid idiot. Wake up and dance in the clarity of perfect contradiction. Come out of the smoke, the world is tossing in its sleep, the sun is up, the land is bursting in the silence of dawn.

The clear bell of Atlas rings once again over the sea, and the animals come to the shore at his feet. The gentle earth relaxes and spreads out to embrace the strong sun. The grasses and flowers speak their own secret names. With his great gentle hands, Atlas opens the clouds—and birds spill back onto the land out of Paradise.

—Raids on the Unspeakable

JUNE 28

Beyond Paradise

We must not imagine Paradise as a place of ease and sensual pleasure. It is a state of peace and rest, by all means, but what the Desert Fathers sought, when they believed they could find "paradise" in the desert, was the lost innocence, the emptiness and purity of heart which had belonged to Adam and Eve in Eden. Evidently, they could not have expected to find beautiful trees and gardens in the waterless desert, burned by the sun. Obviously, they did not expect to find a place, among the fiery rocks and caves, where they could recline at ease in shady groves, by cool running water.

What the Desert Fathers sought was paradise within

themselves, or rather above and beyond themselves. They sought paradise in the recovery of that "unity" which had been shattered by the "knowledge of good and evil."

—*Zen and the Birds of Appetite*

Flight from Disunity

There is only one true flight from the world: it is not an escape from conflict, anguish, and suffering, but the flight from disunity and separation, to unity and peace in the love of other men.

—*New Seeds of Contemplation*

JUNE 29
A Prayer to God the Father

Today, Father, this blue sky lauds you. The delicate green and orange flowers of the tulip poplar tree praise you. The distant blue hills praise you, together with the sweet-smelling air that is full of brilliant light. The bickering flycatchers praise you with the lowing cattle and the quails that whistle over there.

I, too, Father, praise you with all these, my brothers, and they give voice to my own heart and to my own silence. We are all one silence, and a diversity of voices.

If I have any choice to make, it is to live here and perhaps die here. But, in any case, it is not the living or the dying that matter, but speaking your name with confidence in this light, in this unvisited place: to speak your name of "Father" just by being here as "son" in the Spirit and the Light which you have given, and which are no unearthly light, but simply this plain June day, with its shining field, its tulip tree, the pines, the woods, the clouds, and the flowers everywhere.

—*Conjectures of a Guilty Bystander*

JUNE 30

This Is the Land

This is the land where you have given me roots in eternity, O God of heaven and earth. This is the burning promised land, the house of God, the gate of heaven, the place of peace, the place of silence, the place of wrestling with the angel.

The Lord God is present where the new day shines in the moisture on the young grasses. The Lord God is present where the small wildflowers are known to him alone. The Lord God passes suddenly, in the wind, at the moment when night ebbs into the ground.

He who is infinitely great has given his children a share of his own innocence. His alone is the gentlest of loves, whose pure flame respects all things.

Every wave of the sea is free. Every river on earth proclaims its own liberty. The independent trees lift up their leafy heads in peace and exultation. The trees grow the way they like, and all things do the things they do for the pleasure of God.

Yet God does not need to find pleasure in his creation. But we use the word pleasure, and we say he is pleased, because in all these things his liberality and wisdom and mercy take their pleasure in his own infinite freedom.

—*The Sign of Jonas*

July

JULY 1

Rooted in Liberty

It is God's love that warms me in the sun and God's love that sends the cold rain. It is God's love that feeds me in the bread I eat and God that feeds me also by hunger and fasting.

It is the love of God that sends the winter days when I am cold and sick, and the hot summer when I labor and my clothes are full of sweat: but it is God who breathes on me with light winds off the river and in breezes out of the wood.

His love spreads the shade of the sycamore over my head and sends the water-boy along the edge of the wheatfield with a bucket from the spring, while the laborers are resting and the mules stand under the tree.

It is God's love that speaks to me in the birds and streams, and all these things are seeds sent to me from his will. If these seeds would take root in my liberty, and if his will would grow from my freedom, I would become the love that he is, and my harvest would be his glory and my own joy.

—New Seeds of Contemplation

JULY 2

The Realm of Mercy

There is, above the consistent and the logical world of justice, an inconsistent and illogical world where nothing "hangs together," where justice no longer damns each man to his own darkness. This inconsistent world is the realm of mercy.

—Raids on the Unspeakable

JULY 3

Darkness and Silence

The protection of darkness and silence is extremely necessary for the soul that begins to burn with these touches of the spirit of God. For when the soul has thus known God divinely, the memory of the encounter is sometimes stirred up by the lines of Psalms to a blaze that unnerves it beyond its capacity to bear.

In this degree of prayer, there may arise high seas of inspiration that destroy the mind with the weight of a superhuman demand. But we have no help from God to tackle this demand. It is not the wave of his present power, but an undertow that follows after his passing.

Caught in the clenched fist of this bullying sea of love, which is neither human nor divine and which seems to be something elemental in its brutality, we are drawn under and seen to drown until God catches us again and holds us under, not under the sea, but under the mystery of his eternity, where alone there is breathing.

—Bread in the Wilderness

JULY 4

An American Meditation

The attachment of the modern American to his automobile, and the symbolic role played by his car, with its aggressive and lubric design, its useless power, its otiose gadgetry, its consumption of fuel, which is advertised as having almost supernatural power—this is where the study of American mythology should begin.

Meditation on the automobile, what it is used for, what it stands for—the automobile as weapon, as self-advertisement, as brothel, as a means of suicide, etc.—might lead us at once right into the heart of all contemporary American problems: race, war, the crisis of marriage, the flight from reality into myth and fanaticism, the growing brutality and irrationality of American mores.

—Conjectures of a Guilty Bystander

JULY 5

Sanity in Our Time

I am beginning to realize that "sanity" is no longer a value or an end in itself. The "sanity" of modern man is about as useful to him as the huge bulk and muscles of the dinosaur. If modern man were a little less sane, a little more doubtful, a little more aware of his absurdities and contradictions, perhaps there might be a possibility of his survival. But if he is sane, too sane, perhaps we must say that in a society like ours the worst insanity is to be totally without anxiety, totally "sane."

—Raids on the Unspeakable

JULY 6

A Crisis of Truth

It is not by words only that we speak. Our aims, our plans of action, our outlook, our attitudes, our habitual response to the problems and challenges of life, "speak" of our inner being and reveal our fidelity or infidelity to ourselves. Our very existence, our life itself, contains an implicit pretension to meaning, since all our free acts are implicit commitments, selections of "meanings" which we seem to find confronting us. Our very existence is "speech" interpreting reality.

But the crisis of truth in the modern world comes from the bewildering complexity of the almost infinite contradictory propositions and claims to meaning uttered by millions of acts, movements, changes, decisions, attitudes, gestures, events, going on all around us. Most of all, a crisis of truth is precipitated when men realize that almost all these claims are in fact without significance—when they are not, in great part, fraudulent.

—*Seeds of Destruction*

July 7

This Day

A sweet summer afternoon. Cool breezes and a clean sky. This day will not come again.

The young bulls lie under a tree in the corner of their field.

Quiet afternoon. Blue hills. Day lilies nod in the wind. This day will not come again.

—*Conjectures of a Guilty Bystander*

July 8

One's Place on Earth

Yesterday afternoon I went out to the woods. There was a wall of black sky beyond the knobs, to the west, and you could hear thunder growling all the time in the distance. It was very hot and damp, but there was good wind coming from the direction of the storm.

First, I stopped under an oak tree on top of the hill behind

Nally's and sat there looking out at the wide sweep of the valley and the miles of flat woods over toward the straight line of the horizon.

The wind ran over the bent, brown grasses and moved the shoulders of all the green trees, and I looked at the dark mass of woods beyond the distillery, on those hills down to the south of us, and realized that it is when I am with people that I am lonely, and when I am alone I am no longer lonely.

Gethsemani looked beautiful from the hill. It made much more sense in its surroundings. We do not realize our own setting as we ought to: it is important to know where you are put on the face of the earth.

—*The Sign of Jonas*

JULY 9

Pure Hope

We are not perfectly free until we live in pure hope.
—*No Man Is an Island*

JULY 10

A Gathering of Poets

Poets know that the reason for a poem is not discovered until the poem itself exists. The reason for a living act is realized only in the act itself. This meeting (of poets) is a spontaneous explosion of hopes. That is why it is a venture in prophetic poverty, supported and financed by no foundation, organized and publicized by no official group, but a living expression of the belief that there are now in our world new people, new poets, who are not in tutelage to established political systems or cultural structures—whether communist or capitalist—but who dare to hope in their own vision of reality and of the future. This meeting is united in a flame of hope whose temperature has not yet been taken and whose effects have not yet been estimated, because it is a new fire.

—*Raids on the Unspeakable*

JULY 11

The Cautious Writer

If a writer is so cautious that he never writes anything that cannot be criticized, he will never write anything that can be read. If you want to help other people, you have to make up your mind to write things that some men will condemn.

—*New Seeds of Contemplation*

JULY 12

The Writer's Work

How weary I am of being a writer. How necessary it is for monks to work in the fields, in the rain, in the sun, in the mud, in the clay, in the wind: these are our spiritual directors and our novice-masters. They form our contemplation. They instill us with virtue. They make us as stable as the land we live in. You do not get that out of a typewriter.

—*The Sign of Jonas*

JULY 13

True Artistic Freedom

True artistic freedom can never be a matter of sheer will-fulness, or arbitrary posturing. It is the outcome of authentic possibilities, understood and accepted in their own terms, not the refusal of the concrete in favor of the purely "interior." In the last analysis, the only valid witness to the artist's creative freedom is his work itself. The artist builds his own freedom and forms his own artistic conscience by the work of his hands. Only when the work is finished can he tell whether it was done "freely."

—Raids on the Unspeakable

Our True Liberty

Our true liberty is something we must never sacrifice; for if we sacrifice it, we renounce God himself. Only the false spontaneity of caprice, the pseudo-liberty of sin, is to be sacrificed.

—New Seeds of Contemplation

JULY 14

Practical Norms

Warm sun. Perhaps these yellow wildflowers have the minds of little girls. My worship is a blue sky and ten thousand crickets in the deep wet hay of the field. My vow is the silence under their song. I admire the woodpecker and the dove in simple mathematics of flight. Together we study practical norms. The plowed and planted field is red as a

brick in the sun and says: *"Now my turn!"* Several of us begin
to sing.

—Cables to the Ace

JULY 15

Cause of Great Joy

I am finding myself forced to admit that my lamentations
about my writing job have been foolish. At the moment, the
writing is one thing that gives me access to some real silence
and solitude. Also I find that it helps me to pray, because
when I pause at my work I find that the mirror inside me is
surprisingly clean and deep and serene, and God shines
there and is immediately found, without hunting, as if he
had come close to me while I was writing, and I had not
observed his coming. And this, I think, should be the cause
of great joy, and to me it is.

—The Sign of Jonas

JULY 16

Affirmation of God

It seems to me that contemplatives should be able to say to
modern man something about God that answers the pro-
foundly important and significant accusation of Marx against
religion. Marx said religion inevitably leads to the alienation
of man. It is not fulfillment, but opium. Man in his worship of
God divests himself of his own powers and of his own dignity, and attributes these to an invisible and remote God,
and then gets God to grant them, give them back to him, bit
by bit, in retail packages. But that is not the case. We are
learning more and more that the denial of God is really the

denial of man. Yet, on the other hand, the affirmation of God is the true affirmation of man.

—*Contemplation in a World of Action*

JULY 17

Religious Arguments

The arguments of religious men are so often insincere, and their insincerity is proportionate to their anger. Why do we get angry about what we believe? Because we do not really believe it ourselves. Or else what we pretend to be defending as the "truth" is really our own self-esteem. A man of sincerity is less interested in defending the truth than in stating it clearly, for he thinks that if the truth is clearly seen, it can very well take care of itself.

—*No Man Is an Island*

JULY 18

Agony of Ambivalence

Even where totalitarianism has not yet completely wiped out all liberty, men are still subject to the corrupting effect of materialism. The world has always been selfish, but the modern world has lost all ability to control its egoism. And yet, having acquired the power to satisfy its material needs and its desires for pleasures and comfort, it has discovered that these satisfactions are not enough. They do not bring peace, they do not bring happiness. They do not bring security either to the individual or to society.

We live at the precise moment when the exorbitant optimism of the materialist world has plunged into spiritual ruin. We find ourselves living in a society of men who have discovered their own nonentity where they least expected to—in the midst of power and technological achievement. The result is an agony of ambivalence in which each man is forced to project upon his neighbors a burden of self-hatred which is too great to be tolerated by his own soul.

—*The Living Bread*

JULY 19

A Misused Word

Love is, unfortunately, a much misused word. It trips easily off the Christian tongue—so easily that one gets the impression it means others ought to love us for standing on their necks.

—*Faith and Violence*

JULY 20

Money to Burn

Since money is what it is, I do not deny that you may be worthy of all praise if you light your cigarettes with it. That would show you had a deep, pure sense of the ontological value of the dollar. Nevertheless, if that is all you can think of doing with money, you will not long enjoy the advantages that it can still obtain.

—*No Man Is an Island*

JULY 21

The Price of Rain

Let me say this before rain becomes a utility that they can

plan and distribute for money. By "they" I mean the people who cannot understand that rain is a festival, who do not appreciate its gratuity, who think that what has no price has no value, that what cannot be sold is not real, so that the only way to make something actual is to place it on the market. The time will come when they will sell you even your rain. At the moment, it is still free, and I am in it. I celebrate its gratuity and its meaninglessness.

—*Raids on the Unspeakable*

JULY 22
The Only Liberation

To be little, to be nothing, to rejoice in your imperfections, to be glad that you are not worthy of attention, that you are of no account in the universe. This is the only liberation. The only way to true solitude.

—*The Sign of Jonas*

JULY 23
Aware of God's Purity

Very hot. The birds sing and the monks sweat, and about 3:15, when I had just changed all our clothes for the fourth time today and hung out the wet ones to dry, I stood in the doorway of the grand parlor and looked at a huge pile of Kentucky cumulus cloud out beyond Mount Olivet—with a buzzard lazily planing back and forth over the sheep pasture, very high and black against the white mountain of cloud. Blue shadows on the cloud.

At prayer. Aware of God's purity surrounding my own imperfection with purity and peace. Yet helpless to get myself out of the way, so that there could be nothing left but his purity. No other solution but to wait in love and humility— and love my imperfection.

—The Sign of Jonas

JULY 24

Love

O, love, why can't you leave me alone?—which is a rhetorical question meaning: for heaven's sake, don't.

—The Sign of Jonas

JULY 25

A Hidden Answer

Reading Chuang Tzu, I wonder seriously if the wisest answer (on the human level, apart from the answer of faith) is not beyond ethics and politics. It is a hidden answer, it defies analysis and cannot be embodied in a program. Ethics and politics, of course, but only in passing, only as a night's lodging.

There is a time for action, a time for commitment, but never for total involvement in the intricacies of the movement. There is a moment of innocence and *kairos*, when action makes a great deal of sense. But who can recognize such moments? Not he who is debauched by a sense of programs. And when all action has become absurd, shall one continue to act simply because once, a long time ago, it made a great deal of sense? As if one were always getting somewhere?

There is a time to listen, in the active life as everywhere

else, and the better part of action is waiting, not knowing what next, and not having a glib answer.

—Conjectures of a Guilty Bystander

JULY 26
Pacing the Garden

Silence is not necessarily tight-lipped and absolute—the silence of men pacing the garden with puckered brows, ignoring each other—but the tranquility of necessary leisure in which Religious can relax in the peace of a friendly and restful solitude and once again become themselves.

—Contemplation in a World of Action

JULY 27
The Ox Mountain Parable

On Mencius: Note the importance of the "night spirit" and the "dawn breath" in restoring to life the forest that had been cut down.

Even though the Ox Mountain forest has been cut to the ground, if the mountain is left to rest and to recuperate in the night and the dawn, the trees will return. But men cut them down, cattle browse on the new shoots: no night spirit, no dawn breath—no rest, no renewal—and finally one is convinced that there never were any woods on the Ox Mountain.

So, Mencius concludes, with human nature. Without the night spirit, the dawn breath, silence, passivity, rest, man's nature cannot be itself. In its barrenness it is no longer *natura:* nothing grows from it, nothing is born of it anymore.

—Conjectures of a Guilty Bystander

JULY 28

Independent Thought

Someone has to try to keep his head clear of static and preserve the interior solitude and silence that are essential for independent thought.

—*Faith and Violence*

JULY 29

Climate of Penance

I have never sweated so much in my life, even at Gethsemani. The heat has gone on unrelieved for some three weeks. No air. Nothing is dry. Water comes out of you as soon as anything—even the air itself—touches your skin, and you kneel in choir with sweat rolling down your ribs, and you feel as if you were being smothered by a barber with hot towels—only this barber doesn't leave a hole for you to breathe through.

Tides of sweat coming out of you, blinding your face, making your clothes weigh twice their ordinary weight. And yet, somehow, it is good and satisfying to suffer these things and to do some of the penance we are supposed to do; and at night, when we stand in our boiling tunnel and shout our *Salve* at the lighted window, you feel the whole basilica swing with the exultation of the monks and brothers who are dissolving in this humid furnace.

—*The Sign of Jonas*

JULY 30

A Certain Direction

Chuang Tzu said: "At the present time the whole world is under a delusion, and though I may wish to go in a certain direction, how can I succeed in doing so? Knowing that I cannot go that way, to force my way would be another delusion. Therefore, my best course is to let my purpose go and no more pursue it. If I do not pursue it, whom shall I have to share my sorrow?"

—Conjectures of a Guilty Bystander

JULY 31

More Like Eden

It was quiet as the Garden of Eden. I sat on a high bank, under young pines, and looked out over this glen. Right under me was a dry creek, with clean pools lying like glass between the shale pavement of the stream, and the shale was as white and crumpled as sea-biscuit. Down in the glen were the songs of marvelous birds.

I saw the gold-orange flame of an oriole in a tree. Orioles are too shy to come near the monastery. There was a cardinal whistling somewhere, but the best song was that of two birds that sounded as wonderful as nightingales, and their song echoed through the wood. I could not tell what they were. I have never heard such birds before. The echo made the place sound more remote and self-contained, more perfectly enclosed, and more like Eden.

—The Sign of Jonas

August

AUGUST 1

A Season of Effort

Not to be without words in a season of effort. Not to be without a vow in the summer of harvest. What have the signs promised on the lonely hill? Word and work have their measure, and so does pain. Look in your own life and see if you find it.

—*Cables to the Ace*

AUGUST 2

A New Silence

If our life is poured out in useless words, we will never hear anything, will never become anything; and, in the end, because we have said everything before we had anything to say, we shall be left speechless at the moment of our greatest decision.

But silence is order to that final utterance. It is not an end in itself. Our whole life is a meditation of our last decision— the only decision that matters. And we meditate in silence. Yet we are bound, to some extent, to speak to others, to help them see their way to their own decision, to teach them Christ.

In teaching them Christ, our very words teach them a new silence: the silence of the Resurrection. In that silence they are formed and prepared so that they also may speak what they have heard. *I have believed, therefore have I spoken* (Ps. 115:1).

—*Thoughts in Solitude*

AUGUST 3

Swept Clean of Images

How true it is that our knowledge and sense and experience of God are sometimes so much sharper and cleaner when we are uncomfortable and hot and physically cramped and suffering than when we are cool and at rest.

So, though I am always recollected and in God's presence in the woods, and at peace and happy with him, I am in more obscurity when in the hot choir, kneeling before the Blessed Sacrament, on a day of recollection with the sweat pouring down my ribs.

Usually, in any church, my mind is paralyzed with distractions, especially during the evening meditation. Yet how often in the last three minutes of the meditation, my mind will suddenly be swept clean of images and my heart will sink into deep rest in God, and I will be free for that little moment of rest and joy he allows me.

—The Sign of Jonas

AUGUST 4

Getting Things Done

Let us start from one admitted fact: if prayer, meditation, and contemplation were once taken for granted as central realities in human life everywhere, they are so no longer. They are regarded, even by believers, as somehow marginal and secondary. What counts is getting things done.

—Contemplation in a World of Action

AUGUST 5

Harlotries of the Apocalypse

Our idols are by no means dumb and powerless. The sardonic diatribes of the prophets against images of wood and stone do not apply to our images that live, and speak, and smile, and dance, allure us, and lead us off to the kill. Not only are we idolaters, but we are likely to carry out point by point the harlotries of the Apocalypse.

And if we do, we will do so innocently, decently, with clean hands, for the blood is always shed somewhere else! The smoke of the victims is always justified by some clean sociological explanation; and, of course, it is not superstition, because we are by definition the most enlightened people that ever happened.

—Faith and Violence

Sour Grapes

Abbot Moses said: A man who lives apart from other men is like a ripe grape. And a man who lives in the company of others is a sour grape.

—The Wisdom of the Desert

AUGUST 6

Gift of Solitude

Today, more than ever, we need to recognize that the gift of solitude is not ordered to the acquisition of strange contemplative powers, but, first of all, to the recovery of one's deep self, and to the renewal of an authenticity which is presently twisted out of shape by the pretentious routines of a disordered togetherness.

—Contemplation in a World of Action

AUGUST 7

A Moment in Eternity

As soon as a man is fully disposed to be alone with God, he is alone with God no matter where he may be—in the country, the monastery, the woods, or the city.

The lightning flashes from east to west, illuminating the whole horizon and striking where it pleases, and at the same instant the infinite liberty of God flashes in the depths of that man's soul, and he is illumined.

At that moment, he sees that though he seems to be in the middle of his journey, he has already arrived at the end. For the life of grace on earth is the beginning of the life of glory. Although he is a traveler in time, he has opened his eyes— for a moment—in eternity.

—Thoughts in Solitude

AUGUST 8

Fields of Evening

When I walk in the cemetery in the cool evening as the sun is going down—there is almost no sunlight left now in the interval after supper—I think of Isaac, meditating in the fields at evening and of Rebecca coming to marry him, from a far country, riding on a rich camel, sailing across the desert like a queen in a great ship.

—The Sign of Jonas

August 9

Surrounded by Bees

Here I sit surrounded by bees and write in this book. The bees are happy, and therefore they are silent. They are working in the delicate white flowers of the weeds among which I sit. I am on the east side of the house, where I am not as cool as I thought I was going to be, and I sit on top of the bank that looks down over the beehives and the pond, where the ducks used to be, and Rohan's knob in the distance. And that big wobbly step-ladder I nearly fell off, while cleaning the church, stands abandoned out there next to one of the cherry trees, and the branches of a little plum tree before me, right by the road, sag with blue plums.

—*The Sign of Jonas*

August 10

Leaving Things Alone

I know about letting the world alone, not interfering. I do not know about running things. Letting things alone, so that men will not blow their nature out of shape! Not interfering, so that men will not be changed into something they are not! When men do not get twisted and maimed beyond recognition, when they are allowed to live—the purpose of government is achieved.

—*The Way of Chuang Tzu*

August 11
How the Wise Man Governs

The wise man, when he must govern, knows how to do nothing. Letting things alone, he rests in his original nature. He who will govern shall respect the governed no more than he respects himself. If he loves his own person enough to let it rest in its original truth, he will govern others without hurting them.

Let him keep the deep drives in his own guts from going into action. Let him keep still, not looking, not hearing. Let him sit like a corpse, with the dragon power alive all around him.

In complete silence, his voice will be like thunder. His movements will be invisible, like those of a spirit, but the powers of heaven will go with them. Unconcerned, doing nothing, he will see all the things grow ripe around him. Where will he find time to govern?

—The Way of Chuang Tzu

August 12
An Article of Faith

The fact that most men believe—as an article of faith—we are now in a position to solve all our problems does not prove that this is so. On the contrary, this belief is so unfounded that it is itself one of our greatest problems.

—Conjectures of a Guilty Bystander

Christ in Dialogue

Christ is found not in loud and pompous declarations, but in humble and fraternal dialogue.

—Emblems for a Season of Fury

AUGUST 13

A Passion for Unreality

One need not be a monk to turn to the way of contemplation. It is sufficient to be a child of God, a human person. It is enough that one has in oneself the instinct for truth, the desire of that freedom from limitation and from servitude to external things which Saint Paul calls the "servitude of corruption" and which, in fact, holds the whole world of man in bondage by passion, greed, the lust for sensation and for individual survival, as though one could become rich enough, powerful and clever enough, to cheat death.

Unfortunately, this passion for unreality and for the impossible fills the world today with violence, hatred, and, indeed, with a kind of insane and cunning fury which threatens our very existence.

—Faith and Violence

AUGUST 14

Renewed in Scripture

By the reading of Scripture, I am so renewed that all nature seems renewed around me and with me.

The sky seems to be a pure, a cooler blue, the trees a

deeper green, light is sharper on the outlines of the forest and the hills, and the whole world is charged with the glory of God, and I feel fire and music in the earth under my feet.

—*The Sign of Jonas*

AUGUST 15

The Cornfield

How high the corn is this summer! What joy there is in seeing the tall crests nod ten and twelve feet above the ground, and the astounding size of the silk-bearded ears! You come down out of the novitiate, through the door in the enclosure wall, over the little bridge, and down into this paradise of tall stalks and leaves and silence. There is a sacredness about the beauty of tall maize, and I understand how the Mayas must have felt about it: in this feeling there is a pre-Eucharistic rightness and wisdom. How can we not love such things?

—*Conjectures of a Guilty Bystander*

Primacy of Love

Love, in fact, is the spiritual life; and, without it, all other exercises of the spirit, however lofty, are emptied of content and become mere illusions. The more lofty they are, the more dangerous the illusion.

—*The Wisdom of the Desert*

AUGUST 16

A False Blaze

Even when we enter into the contemplative life, we still

carry our passions and our sensible nature along with us like a store of unprotected gasoline. And sometimes the sparks that fly in the pure darkness of a contemplation get into that fuel by accident and start a blaze in the emotions and the senses. This blaze flares up and burns out in a few moments.

—*New Seeds of Contemplation*

AUGUST 17

In the Spiritual Life

I made a beeline for the little grove of cedars that is behind the old horsebarn and crowded up against the far end of the enclosure wall, and it was nice. By the long time it took me to get completely recollected, I realized that I have been awfully busy and my mind is terribly active. And if I had to give an account of my stewardship, I would have to fall upon God's mercy more heavily than ever, because it seems to me that since I became a great success in the book business I have been becoming more and more of a failure in my vocation.

Not that I haven't made efforts to keep my head above water; but in the spiritual life it is not so hard to drown, when you imagine you are swimming.

—*The Sign of Jonas*

AUGUST 18

Presumptuous Visionaries

The spiritual cataclysms that sometimes overtook some of the presumptuous visionaries of the desert are there to show the dangers of the lonely life—like bones whitening in the sand.

—*The Wisdom of the Desert*

Full of Reality

Love cannot come of emptiness. It is full of reality.

—Emblems for a Season of Fury

AUGUST 19

Images of the World

As usual, one comes back to the old question: what do you mean by "the world," anyway? In this, I don't think an abstract answer makes too much sense. My concrete answer is: the image of a society that is happy because it drinks Coca-Cola or Seagrams, or both, and is protected by the Bomb. The society that is imaged in the mass media and in advertising, in the movies, in TV, in best-sellers, in current fads, in all the pompous and trifling masks with which it hides callousness, sensuality, hypocrisy, cruelty, and fear. Is this "the world?" Yes. It is the same wherever you have mass man—the same spiritual cretinism which in fact makes Christians and atheists indistinguishable.

—Contemplation in a World of Action

AUGUST 20

Dazzled with Slogans

We live in a society that tries to keep us dazzled with euphoria in a bright cloud of lively and joy-loving slogans. Yet nothing is more empty and more dead, nothing is more insultingly insincere and destructive than the vapid grins on the billboards and the moronic beatitudes in the magazines, which assure us that we are all in bliss right now. I know, of course, that we are fools, but I do not think any of us are fools enough to believe that we are now in heaven.

—Faith and Violence

AUGUST 21

A Kind of Death

Love demands a complete inner transformation, for without this we cannot possibly come to identify ourselves with our brother. We have to become, in some sense, the person we love. And this involves a kind of death of our own being, our own self. No matter how hard we try, we resist this death: we fight back with anger, with recriminations, with demands, with ultimatums. We seek any convenient excuse to break off and give up the difficult task.

—The Wisdom of the Desert

AUGUST 22

Saint Bernard's Day

The really hot weather stopped all of a sudden the evening before Saint Bernard's day, but prickly heat tends to be especially sharp when you are cooling off.

On Saint Bernard's day—I sat up on the hill behind Nally's, not wanting to walk far into the woods, because the more time you spend walking, the less you have for really deep prayer. So I looked at the great big sweep of country and that far line of hills that is steeped in spiritual associations for me, and at the abbey and the church sitting in the carpet of fields like a reliquary, and which contain all that is

most precious in the world, the Body of Christ, and His
Divinity, the Living God.

—The Sign of Jonas

AUGUST 23

A Sign of Contradiction

The Cross is the sign of contradiction—destroying the seriousness of the Law, of the Empire, of the armies, of blood
sacrifice, and of obsession.

But the magicians keep turning the Cross to their own
purposes. Yes, it is for them, too, a sign of contradiction: the
awful blasphemy of the religious magician who makes the
Cross contradict mercy! This, of course, is the ultimate
temptation of Christianity! To say that Christ has locked all
the doors, has given one answer, settled everything and
departed, leaving all life enclosed in the frightful consistency of a system outside of which there is seriousness and
damnation, inside of which there is the intolerable flippancy
of the saved—while nowhere is there any place left for the
mystery of the freedom of divine mercy, which alone is truly
serious and worthy of being taken seriously.

—Raids on the Unspeakable

AUGUST 24

A Questioning Faith

You cannot be a man of faith unless you know how to
doubt. You cannot believe in God unless you are capable of
questioning the authority of prejudice, even though that
prejudice seems to be religious. Faith is not blind conformity
to a prejudice—a "pre-judgment." It is a decision, a judg-

ment that is fully and deliberately taken in the light of a truth that cannot be proven.

—*New Seeds of Contemplation*

AUGUST 25

A True Memory

Memory is corrupted and ruined by a crowd of "memories." If I am going to have a true memory, there are a thousand things that must first be forgotten. Memory is not fully itself when it reaches only into the past. A memory that is not alive to the present does not "remember" the here and now, does not "remember" its true identity, is not memory at all. He who remembers nothing but facts and past events, and is never brought back into the present, is a victim of amnesia.

—*New Seeds of Contemplation*

AUGUST 26

Your Original Name

Take thought, man, tonight. Take thought, man, tonight when it is dark, when it is raining. Take thought of the game you have forgotten. You are the child of a great and peaceful race. You are the son of an unutterable fable. You were discovered on a mild mountain. You have come up out of the godlike ocean. You are holy, disarmed, signed with a chaste emblem. You are also marked with forgetfulness. Deep inside your breast you wear the number of loss. Take thought, man, tonight. Do this. Do this. Recover your original name.

—*Raids on the Unspeakable*

AUGUST 27

Exiled from Self

Solitude means being lonely, not in a way that pleases you, but in a way that frightens and empties you to the extent that it means being exiled even from yourself.

—*The Sign of Jonas*

AUGUST 28

Flight into the Desert

If we reflect a moment, we will see that to fly into the desert in order to be extraordinary is only to carry the world with you as an implicit standard of comparison. The result would be nothing but self-contemplation, or self-comparison with the negative standard of the world one has abandoned. Some of the monks of the desert did this, as a matter of fact, and the only fruit of their trouble was that they went out of their heads.

The simple men who lived their lives out to a good old age among the rocks and sands only did so because they had come into the desert to be themselves, their ordinary selves, and to forget a world that divided them from themselves. There can be no other valid reason for seeking solitude or for leaving the world. And thus to leave the world is, in fact, to help save it in saving oneself.

—*The Wisdom of the Desert*

AUGUST 29

Beyond Everything

Our destiny is to go on beyond everything, to leave everything, to press forward to the End and find in the End our Beginning, the ever-new Beginning that has no End.

—Conjectures of a Guilty Bystander

AUGUST 30

Drugged with Happiness

In the afternoon I went out to the old horsebarn with the Book of Proverbs and, indeed, with the whole Bible, and I was wandering around in the hay loft, where there is a big gap in the roof, and one of the rotting floorboards gave way under me and I nearly fell through.

Afterwards, I sat and looked out at the hills and the gray clouds and couldn't read anything. When the flies got too bad, I wandered across the bare pasture and sat by the enclosure wall, perched on the edge of a ruined bathtub that has been placed there for the horses to drink out of. A pipe comes through the wall and plenty of water flows in the bathtub from a spring somewhere in the woods, and I couldn't read there either.

I just listened to the clean water flowing and looked at the wreckage of the horsebarn on top of the bare knoll in front of me, and remained drugged with happiness and with prayer.

—The Sign of Jonas

AUGUST 31

The Common Celebration

Christian personalism does not require that the inmost secret of our being become manifest or public to all. We do not even have to see it clearly ourselves! We are more truly

Christian persons when our inmost secret remains a mystery shared by ourselves and God, and communicated to others in a way that is at the same time secret and public.

In other words, Christian personalism does not root out the inner secret of the individual in order to put it on display in a spiritual beauty contest. On the contrary, our growing awareness of our own personality enables us at the same time to divine and to respect the inner secret of our neighbor, our brother in Christ.

Christian personalism is, then, the sacramental sharing of the inner secret of personality in the mystery of love. In fact, Christian personalism is the discovery of one's own inmost self, and of the inmost self of one's neighbor, in the mystery of Christ: a discovery that respects the hiddenness and incommunicability of each one's personal secret, while paying tribute to his presence in the common celebration.

—*Seasons of Celebration*

September

SEPTEMBER 1

Work or Agitation?

Work occupies the body and the mind and is necessary for the health of the spirit. Work can help us to pray and be recollected, if we work properly. Agitation, however, destroys the spiritual usefulness of work and even tends to frustrate its physical and social purpose. Agitation is the useless and ill-directed action of the body. It expresses the inner confusion of a soul without peace.

Work brings peace to the soul that has a semblance of order and spiritual understanding. Agitation—a condition of spirit that is quite normal in the world of business—is the fruit of tension in a spirit that is turning dizzily from one stimulus to another and trying to react to fifteen different appeals at the same time. Under the surface of agitation, and furnishing it with its monstrous and inexhaustible drive, is the force of fear or elemental greed for money, or pleasure, or power. The more complex a man's passion, the more complex his agitation.

All this is the death of the interior life. Occasional church-going and the recitation of hasty prayers have no power to cleanse this purulent wound.

—*No Man Is an Island*

SEPTEMBER 2

Things Ill-Made

Where we find buildings that are ugly, furniture ill-made, doors that do not close properly, vines and fruit trees clumsily pruned, materials and fodder going to waste, the lack of skill and care which these things represent might simply be the fruit of a wrong attitude toward work itself.

—The Silent Life

SEPTEMBER 3

End of Summer

This morning, under a cobalt blue sky, summer having abruptly ended, I am beginning the Book of Job. It is not warm enough to sit for long in the shade of the cedars. The woods are crisply outlined in the sun, and the clamor of distant crows is sharp in the air that no longer sizzles with locusts. And Job moves me deeply. This year, more than ever, it has a special poignancy.

I now know that all my own poems about the world's suffering have been inadequate: they have not solved anything, they have only camouflaged the problem. And it seems to me that the urge to write a real poem about suffering and sin is only another temptation, because, after all, I do not really understand.

—The Sign of Jonas

SEPTEMBER 4

The Realm of Waste

The realm of politics is the realm of waste. The Pharaohs at least built pyramids. With the labor of hundreds and thousands of slaves, they built temples, and they built pyramids. Perhaps in a certain sense this labor was wasted; yet it has meaning, and its meaning remains powerful and eloquent, if mysterious, after centuries. The work of the slaves was forced, it was cruel, but it was work. It still had a kind of human dimension. There was something of grandeur about it. The slaves lived, and saw "their" pyramids grow.

Our century is not a century of pyramids, but of extermination camps, in which man himself is purely and deliberately wasted; and the sardonic gesture, saving the hair, the teeth, and the clothes of the victims, is simply a way of pointing to the wasting of humanity.

It was a way of saying: "These people, whom you think to be persons, whom you are tempted to value as having souls, as being spiritual, these are nothing. We are so much better and more human than they that we can afford to destroy a whole man in order to make a lampshade out of his skin. He is nothing!"

—Conjectures of a Guilty Bystander

SEPTEMBER 5

A Pragmatic Policy

One of our most important tasks today is to clear the atmosphere so that men can understand their plight without hatred, without fury, without desperation, and with the minimum of goodwill. A humble and objective seriousness is necessary for the long task of restoring mutual confidence and preparing the way for the necessary work of collaboration in building world peace. This restoration of a climate of relative sanity is perhaps more important than specific decisions regarding the morality of this or that strategy, this or that pragmatic policy.

—Seeds of Destruction

SEPTEMBER 6

Communion of Silence

The solitary life, being silent, clears away the smokescreen of words that man has laid down between his mind and things. In solitude we remain face to face with the naked being of things. And yet we find that the nakedness of reality, which we have feared, is neither a matter of terror nor of shame. It is clothed in the friendly communion of silence, and this silence is related to love. The world our words have attempted to classify, to control and even to despise (because they could not contain it), comes close to us, for silence teaches us to know reality by respecting it where words have defiled it.

—Thoughts in Solitude

SEPTEMBER 7

To Be a Saint

If I am to be a saint—and there is nothing else that I can think of desiring to be—it seems that I must get there by writing books in a Trappist monastery. If I am to be a saint, I have not only to be a monk, which is what all monks must do to become saints, but I must also put down on paper what I have become. It may sound simple, but it is not an easy vocation.

To be as good a monk as I can, and to remain myself, and to write about it: to put myself down on paper, in such a situation, with the most complete simplicity and integrity, masking nothing, confusing no issues. This is very hard, because I am all mixed up in illusions and attachments. But no need for breast-beating and lamentation before the eyes of anyone but you, O God, who see the depths of my fatuity.

To be frank without being boring. It is a kind of crucifixion. Not a very dramatic or painful one. But it requires so much honesty that it is beyond my nature. It must come somehow from the Holy Spirit.

—The Sign of Jonas

SEPTEMBER 8

Sound of the Earth

Morning. Good for foliage to resist the faithful wind. Lean into a new light. Listen to well-ordered hills go by, rank upon rank, in the sun. The heat will soon blaze blue and white. The long frying of September in the shallow pan of the fields. The sound of the earth goes up to embrace the constant sky. My own center is the teeming heart of natural families.

—Cables to the Ace

SEPTEMBER 9

The Inmost Ground

The world cannot be a problem to anyone who sees that ultimately Christ, the world, his brother and his own inmost ground are made one and the same in grace and redemptive love. If all the current talk about the world helps people to discover this, then it is fine. But if it produces nothing but a whole new divisive gamut of obligatory positions and "contemporary answers," we might as well forget it.

The world itself is no problem, but we are a problem to ourselves because we are alienated from ourselves, and this alienation is due precisely to an inveterate habit of division by which we break reality into pieces and then wonder why, after we have manipulated the pieces until they fall apart, we find ourselves out of touch with life, with reality, with the world, and most of all with ourselves.

—*Contemplation in a World of Action*

SEPTEMBER 10

Obligatory Answers

I have a profound mistrust of all obligatory answers. The great problem of our time is not to formulate clear answers to neat theoretical questions, but to tackle the self-destructive alienation of man in a society dedicated in theory to human values and in practice to the pursuit of power for its own sake. All the new and fresh answers in the world, all the bright official confidence in the collectivity of the secular city, will do nothing to change the reality of this alienation.

The Marxist worldview is the one really coherent and systematic one that has, so far, come forward to replace the old medieval Christian and classic synthesis. It has, in fact, got itself accepted, for better or for worse, by more than half the human race. And yet, while claiming to offer man hope of deliverance from alienation, it has demanded a more unquestioning, a more irrational and a more submissive obedience than ever to its obligatory answers, even when these are manifestly self-contradictory and destructive of the very values they claim to defend.

—*Contemplation in a World of Action*

SEPTEMBER 11

Lovelessness

Lovelessness cannot be kept hidden, because a loveless life is essentially unhappy, frustrated, and destructive.
                    —*Contemplation in a World of Action*

SEPTEMBER 12

The Dry Period

It is not much fun to live the spiritual life with the spiritual equipment of an artist. Yesterday afternoon, in the cornfield, I began to feel rather savage about the whole business. I suppose this irritation was the sign that the dry period was reaching its climax and was about to go over again into the awful battle with joy. My soul was cringing and doubling up and subconsciously getting ready for the next tidal wave. At the moment, all I had left in my heart was an abyss of self-hatred—waiting for the next appalling sea.
                    —*The Sign of Jonas*

SEPTEMBER 13

Surrounded by Beauty

You flowers and trees, you hills and streams, you fields, flocks and wild birds, you books, you poems, and you people, I am unutterably alone in the midst of you. The irrational hunger that sometimes gets into the depths of my will, tries to swing my deepest self away from God and direct it to your love. I try to touch you with the deep fire that is in the center of my heart, but I cannot touch you without defiling both you and myself, and I am abashed, solitary and helpless, surrounded by a beauty that can never belong to me. . . .

—The Sign of Jonas

SEPTEMBER 14

An Unspeakable Reverence

. . . But this sadness generates within me an unspeakable reverence for the holiness of created things, for they are pure and perfect and they belong to God, and they are mirrors of his beauty. He is mirrored in all things, like sunlight in clean water: but if I try to drink the light that is in the water, I only shatter the reflection.

And so I live alone and chaste in the midst of the holy beauty of all created things, knowing that nothing I can see or hear or touch will ever belong to me, ashamed of my absurd need to give myself away to any one of them, or to all of them. The silly, hopeless passion to give myself away to any beauty eats out my heart. It is an unworthy desire, but I cannot avoid it. It is in the hearts of us all, and we have to bear with it, suffer its demands with patience, until we die and go to heaven, where all things will belong to us in their highest causes.

—The Sign of Jonas

SEPTEMBER 15

Moment to Moment

From moment to moment I remember with astonishment

that I am at the same time empty and full, and satisfied because I am empty. I lack nothing. The Lord rules me.

—Conjectures of a Guilty Bystander

SEPTEMBER 16

Active Life

Those who are caught in the machinery of power take no joy except in activity and change—the whirring of the machine! Whenever an occasion for action presents itself, they are compelled to act. They cannot help themselves. They are inexorably moved, like the machine of which they are a part. Prisoner in the world of objects, they have no choice but to submit to the demands of matter. They are pressed down and crushed by external forces, fashion, the market, events, public opinion. Never in a whole lifetime do they recover their right mind! The active life! What a pity!

—The Way of Chuang Tzu

SEPTEMBER 17

Why All the Fuss?

Of all the beings that exist (and there are millions), man is only one. Among all the millions of men that live on earth, the civilized people that live by farming are only a small proportion. Smaller still the number of those who, having office or fortune, travel by carriage or by boat. And of all these, one man in his carriage is nothing more than the tip of a hair on a horse's flank. Why, then, all the fuss about great men and great offices? Why all the disputations of scholars? Why all the wrangling of politicians?

—The Way of Chuang Tzu

SEPTEMBER 18

Haranguing

Pontiffs! Pontiffs! We are all pontiffs haranguing one another, brandishing our croziers at one another, dogmatizing, threatening anathemas!

—*Contemplation in a World of Action*

SEPTEMBER 19

Paying for Insults

Once there was a disciple of a Greek philosopher who was commanded by his Master for three years to give money to everyone who insulted him. When this period of trial was over, the Master said to him: Now you can go to Athens and learn wisdom. When the disciple was entering Athens, he met a certain wise man who sat at the gate insulting everybody who came and went. He also insulted the disciple, who immediately burst out laughing. Why do you laugh when I insult you? said the wise man. Because, said the disciple, for three years I have been paying for this kind of thing, and now you give it to me for nothing. Enter the city, said the wise man, it is all yours. Abbot John used to tell the above story, saying: This is the door of God by which our father, rejoicing in many tribulations, enters into the City of Heaven.

—*The Wisdom of the Desert*

SEPTEMBER 20

The Simplicity of God

No matter how simple discourse may be, it is never simple enough. No matter how simple thought may be, it is never simple enough. No matter how simple love may be, it is never simple enough. The only thing left is the simplicity of the soul in God—or, better, the simplicity of God.

—The Sign of Jonas

SEPTEMBER 21

The Psalms

The Psalms are more than language. They contain within themselves the silence of high mountains and the silence of heaven. It is only when we stand at the bottom of the mountain that it is hard for us to distinguish the language of the Psalter from the tongues of this earth: for Christ must still perforce travel among us as a pilgrim disguised in our own tattered garments.

The Psalter only truly begins to speak and sing within us when we have been led by God and lifted up by him, and have ascended into its silences. When this is done, the Psalms themselves become the Tabernacle of God in which we are protected forever from the rage of the city of business, from the racket of human opinions, from the wild carnival we carry in our hearts, and which the ancient saints called Babylon.

—Bread in the Wilderness

SEPTEMBER 22

The Good News

What makes the Gospel news? The faith, which is created in us by God and with which we hear it as news. This acceptance of the faith, this new birth in the Spirit, opens up a new dimension in which time and eternity meet, in which all things are made new: eternity, time, our own self, the world around us.

—*Conjectures of a Guilty Bystander*

SEPTEMBER 23

Beyond Poetry and Art

Poetry, music, and art have something in common with the contemplative experience. But contemplation is beyond aesthetic intuition, beyond art, beyond poetry. Indeed, it is also beyond philosophy, beyond speculative theology. It resumes, transcends, and fulfills them all; and yet, at the same time, it seems in a certain way to supersede and to deny them all.

Contemplation is always beyond our own knowledge, beyond our own light, beyond systems, beyond explanations, beyond discourse, beyond dialogue, and beyond our own self. To enter into the realm of contemplation, one must, in a certain sense, die: but this death is, in fact, the entrance into a higher life. It is a death for the sake of life, which leaves behind all that we can know or treasure as life, as thought, as experience, as joy, as being.

—*New Seeds of Contemplation*

SEPTEMBER 24

To Speak like God

Reading ought to be an act of homage to the God of all truth.

Books can speak to us like God, like men, or like the noise of the city we live in. They speak to us like God when they bring us light and peace and fill us with silence. They speak to us like God when we desire never to leave them. They speak to us like men when we desire to hear them again. They speak to us like the noise of the city when they hold us captive by a weariness that tells us nothing, gives us no peace, and no support, nothing to remember, and yet will not let us escape.

Books that speak like God speak with too much authority to entertain us. Those that speak like good men hold us by their human charm; we grow by finding ourselves in them. They teach us to know ourselves better by recognizing ourselves in one another.

Books that speak like the noise of multitudes reduce us to despair by the sheer weight of their emptiness. They entertain us like the lights of the city streets at night, by hopes they cannot fulfill.

—*Thoughts in Solitude*

SEPTEMBER 25

Let It Be

Dark dawn. Streaks of pale red, under a few high clouds. A pattern of clotheslines, clothespins, shadowy saplings. Abstraction. There is no way to capture it. Let it be.

—*Conjectures of a Guilty Bystander*

Point Vierge

The first chirps of the waking-day birds mark the *point vierge* of the dawn under a sky as yet without real light, a moment of awe and inexpressible innocence, when the Father in perfect silence opens their eyes.

—Conjectures of a Guilty Bystander

SEPTEMBER 26

John 6

Morning after morning I try to study the sixth chapter of Saint John, and it is too great. I cannot study it. I simply sit still and try to breathe.

There is a small black lizard with a blue, metallic tail, scampering up the yellow wall of the church next to the niche where the Little Flower, with a confidential and rather pathetic look in her eye, offers me a rose. I am glad of the distraction, because now I can breathe again and think a little.

It does no good to use big words to talk about Christ. Since I seem to be incapable of talking about him in the language of a child, I have reached the point where I can scarcely talk about him at all. All my words fill me with shame.

—The Sign of Jonas

SEPTEMBER 27

These Are Good

The silence of the forest, the peace of the early morning

wind moving the branches of the trees, the solitude and isolation of the house of God: these are good because it is in silence, and not in commotion, in solitude and not in crowds, that God best likes to reveal himself most intimately to men.

The humble work in the fields, the labor in the shops, kitchens and bakeries, is good because it divides and disperses the burdens of material life, distributes the cares and responsibilities, so that no one monk has too many material things to think about. Each one contributes his share in peace and recollection, without undue anxiety.

—The Silent Life

SEPTEMBER 28

A Prayer

Lady, Queen of Heaven, pray me into solitude and silence and unity, that all my ways may be immaculate in God.

Let me be content with whatever darkness surrounds me, finding Him always by me, in His mercy.

Let me keep silence in this world, except insofar as God wills, and in the way He wills it.

Let me at least disappear into the writing I do. It should mean nothing special to me, nor harm my recollection. This work could be a prayer; its results should not concern me.

—The Sign of Jonas

SEPTEMBER 29

The Eight Delights

You train your eye, and your vision lusts after color. You train your ear, and you long for delightful sound. You delight in doing good, and your natural kindness is blown out of shape. You delight in righteousness, and you become righteous beyond all reason. You overdo liturgy, and you turn into a ham actor. Overdo your love of music, and you play corn. Love of wisdom leads to wise contriving. Love of knowledge leads to faultfinding.

If men would stay as they really are, taking or leaving these eight delights would make no difference. But if they will not rest in their right state, the eight delights develop like malignant tumors. The world falls into confusion. Since men honor these delights and lust after them, the world has gone stone-blind.

When the delight is over, they still will not let go of it: they surround its memory with ritual worship, they fall on their knees to talk about it, play music and sing, fast and discipline themselves in honor of the eight delights. When the delights become a religion, how can you control them?

—*The Way of Chuang Tzu*

September 30

Love Sails Me Around

Love sails me around the house. I walk two steps on the ground and four steps in the air. It is love. It is consolation. I don't care if it is consolation. I am not attached to consolation. I love God. Love carries me all around. I don't want to *do* anything but love.

And when the bell rings, it is like pulling teeth to make myself shift because of that love, secret love, hidden love, obscure love, down inside me and outside me, where I don't care to talk about it. Anyway, I don't have the time or the energy to discuss such matters. I have only time for eternity, which is to say, for love, love, love.

Maybe Saint Teresa would like to have me snap out of it, but it is pure, I tell you: I am not attached to it (I hope) and it is love, and it gives me soft punches all the time in the center of my heart. Love is pushing me around the monastery, love is kicking me all around, like a gong, I tell you. Love is the only thing that makes it possible for me to continue to tick.

—*The Sign of Jonas*

October

OCTOBER 1

Inner Climate

The change in my own inner climate: the coming of autumn. I am still too young to be thinking about "old age." Really, these years, when you approach fifty and get ready to turn the corner, are supposed to be the best in your life. And I think that is true. I do not say that, for me, they have been the easiest. The change that is working itself out in me comes to the surface of my psyche in the form of deep upheavals of impatience, resentment, disgust.

And yet I am a joyful person. I like life, and I have really nothing to complain of. Then, suddenly, a tide of this unexpected chill comes up out of the depths; and I breathe the cold air of darkness, the sense of void! I recognize it, all right, but it does not bother me. And I say to my body: "Oh, all right, then *die,* you idiot." But that is not what it is trying to do. It is my impatience that thinks of this in terms of death. My body is not sending up signals of emergency and of death; it is only saying: "Let's go a little slower for a change."

—*Conjectures of a Guilty Bystander*

OCTOBER 2

A Very Quiet Evening

Now a beautiful yellow rosebush has filled with flowers. They stand before me like something very precious in the late slanting sun as I write. The evening is very quiet. The crosses in the cemetery are all absolutely motionless, of course. And yet it is as though I had been expecting them to turn to me and speak.

—*The Sign of Jonas*

OCTOBER 3

The Desert of Desolation

Let us never forget that the ordinary way to contemplation lies through a desert without trees and without beauty and without water. The spirit enters a wilderness and travels blindly in directions that seem to lead away from vision, away from God, away from all fulfillment and joy. It may become almost impossible to believe that this road goes anywhere at all, except to a desolation full of dry bones—the ruin of all our hopes and good intentions.

The prospect of this wilderness is something that so appalls most men that they refuse to enter upon its burning sands and travel among its rocks. They cannot believe that contemplation and sanctity are to be found in a desolation where there is no food and no shelter and no refreshment for their imagination and intellect and for the desires of their nature.

—*New Seeds of Contemplation*

OCTOBER 4

True Bread

Take the enjoyment of our daily bread. Bread is true, isn't it? Well, I don't know. Maybe one of the troubles with modern life is that bread is no longer true bread. But around here, in this monastery, we have good bread.

Things that are good are good; and if one is responding to that goodness, one is in contact with a truth from which one is getting something. The truth is doing us good. The truth of the sunshine, the truth of the rain, the truth of the fresh air, the truth of the wind in the trees, these are *truths*. And they are always accessible!

Let us be exposed to these in such a way that they do us good, because these are very accessible forms of truth; and if we allow ourselves to be benefited by the forms of truth that are really accessible to us, instead of rejecting and disparaging and despising them as "merely natural," we will be in a better position to profit by higher forms of truth when they come our way.

—*Contemplation in a World of Action*

OCTOBER 5

On Arguing

Abbot Pastor said: Get away from any man who always argues every time he talks.

—*The Wisdom of the Desert*

OCTOBER 6

Mahatma Gandhi

Gandhi recognized, as no other world leader of our time has done, the necessity to be free from the pressures, the exorbitant and tyrannical demands of a society that is violent because it is essentially greedy, lustful, and cruel. Therefore, he fasted, observed days of silence, lived frequently in retreat, knew the value of solitude, as well as of the totally generous expenditure of his time and energy in listening to others and communicating with them. He recognized the impossibility of being a peaceful and nonviolent man, if one submits passively to the insatiable requirements of a society maddened by overstimulation and obsessed with the demons of noise, voyeurism, and speed.

Gandhi believed that the central problem of our time was the acceptance or the rejection of a basic law of love and truth which had been made known to the world in traditional religions and most clearly by Jesus Christ. Gandhi himself expressly and very clearly declared himself an adherent of this one law. His whole life, his political action, finally even his death, were nothing but a witness to this commitment: "If love is not the law of our being, the whole of my argument falls to pieces."

—*Seeds of Destruction*

OCTOBER 7

The Inner Door

What is the use of my complaining about not being a contemplative, if I do not take the opportunities I get for contemplation? I suppose I take them, but in the wrong way. I spend the time looking for something to read about contemplation—something to satisfy my raffish spiritual appetites—instead of shutting up and emptying my mind and leaving the inner door open for the Holy Spirit to enter from the inside, all the doors being barred and all my blinds down.

—*The Sign of Jonas*

OCTOBER 8

Presence of Evil

The mystic and the spiritual men who in our day remain indifferent to the problems of their fellowmen, who are not fully capable of facing these problems, will find themselves inevitably involved in the same ruin. They will suffer the same deceptions, be implicated in the same crimes. They will go down to ruin with the same blindness and with the same insensitivity to the presence of evil. They will be deaf to the voice crying in the wilderness, for they will have listened to some other, more comforting, voice of their own contrivance.

—Faith and Violence

Difficult

It is not complicated to lead the spiritual life, but it is difficult.

—The Sign of Jonas

OCTOBER 9

In the Sun

I have noticed that when your mind is utterly dead around the house and in church, you can go out to work and soon find God within you after you have been sweating a little in the sun.

—The Sign of Jonas

OCTOBER 10

A Conquered Paradise

Somehow it has been forgotten that a paradise that can be conquered and acquired by force is not paradise at all.

So the story of man's pilgrimage and search has reached the end of a cycle and is starting on another: now that it is clear that there is no paradise on earth that is not defiled, as well as limited, now that there are no lost islands, there is perhaps some dry existentialist paradise of clean ashes to be discovered and colonized in outer space— a "new beginning" that initiates nothing and is little more than a sign of irreversible decision to be disgusted with the paradises and pilgrimages of earth.

Disgust with paradise, but not with crusades! The new planet is apparently to be the base for a more definitive extermination of infidels, together with the mass of less agile pilgrims so occupied in keeping body and soul together that they cannot be singled out as pilgrims to a promised land.

—Mystics and Zen Masters

OCTOBER 11

Crossing the Abyss

What can we gain by sailing to the moon if we are not able to cross the abyss that separates us from ourselves? This is the most important of all voyages of discovery, and without it all the rest are not only useless but disastrous.

Proof: the great travelers and colonizers of the Renaissance were, for the most part, men who perhaps were capable of the things they did precisely because they were alienated from themselves. In subjugating primitive worlds they only imposed on them, with the force of cannons, their own confusion and their own alienation.

—The Wisdom of the Desert

OCTOBER 12

Disguised as Virtue

Some people think it is enough to have one virtue, like

kindness or broadmindedness or charity, and let everything else go. But if you are unselfish in one way and selfish in twenty-five other ways, your virtue will not do you much good. In fact, it will probably turn out to be nothing more than a twenty-sixth variety of the same selfishness, disguised as virtue.

Therefore, do not think that because you seem to have some good quality, all the evil in you can be excused or forgotten on that account alone.

—*New Seeds of Contemplation*

Right Action

A right intention aims only at right action.

—*No Man Is an Island*

OCTOBER 13

On Knowing One's Power

One of the brethren asked an elder, saying: Father, do the holy men always know when the power of God is in them? And the elder replied: No, they do not always know it. For once a very great hermit had a disciple who did something wrong, and the hermit said to him: Go and drop dead! Instantly, the disciple fell down dead. The hermit, overcome with terror, prayed to the Lord, saying: Lord Jesus Christ, I beg Thee to bring my disciple back to life, and from now on I will be careful what I say. Then, right away, the disciple was restored to life.

—*The Wisdom of the Desert*

October 14
A Patchwork of Desires

Soon you will have no interior life at all. Your whole existence will be a patchwork of confused desires and daydreams and velleities in which you do nothing except defeat the work of grace: for all this is an elaborate subconscious device of your own nature to resist God, whose work in your soul demands the sacrifice of all that you desire and delight in, and, indeed, of all that you are.

So keep still, and let him do some work.

This is what it means to renounce not only pleasures and possessions but even your own self.

—New Seeds of Contemplation

October 15
Landscape of Psalms

All the hills and woods are red and brown and copper, and the sky is clear, with one or two very small clouds. A buzzard comes by and investigates me, but I am not dead yet. The whole landscape of woods and hills is getting to be saturated with my prayers and with the Psalms and with the book I read out here under the trees, looking over the wall, not at the world, but at our forest, our solitude.

—The Sign of Jonas

October 16
Lamenting Thoreau

I have read a little of Thoreau and know enough to lament

that such good sense died so long ago. But it could still be ours if only we wanted it. We do not, we want the image, the consuming image, the dead one into which we pour soft drinks. The smiles of the image. All the girls are laughing because the hero-image has a soft drink. He will, with the power of the drink, explode a moon.

So let the moons explode and the books be silent. Let the captains whirl in the sky, let the monkeys in the heavens move levers with hands and feet, and with their big toe explode cities, for a soft drink.

—Seeds of Destruction

OCTOBER 17

A Deepening Present

Solitude is not found so much by looking outside the boundaries of your dwelling as by staying within them. Solitude is not something you must hope for in the future. Rather, it is a deepening of the present; and unless you look for it in the present, you will never find it.

—The Sign of Jonas

Experience

A certain depth of disciplined experience is a necessary ground for fruitful action.

—Contemplation in a World of Action

OCTOBER 18

Autumn Floods

The autumn floods had come. Thousands of wild torrents poured furiously into the Yellow River. It surged and flooded its banks until, looking across, you could not tell an ox from a horse on the other side. Then the River God laughed, delighted to think that all the beauty in the world had fallen into his keeping. So downstream he swung, until he came to the Ocean. There he looked out over the waves, toward the empty horizon in the east, and his face fell. Gazing out at the far horizon, he came to his senses and murmured to the Ocean God: "Well, the proverb is right. He who has got himself a hundred ideas thinks he knows more than anybody else. Such a one am I. Only now do I see what they mean by EXPANSE!"

—The Way of Chuang Tzu

OCTOBER 19

A Lasting City

In the tempest, I have discovered once again—but this time with a peculiarly piercing sharpness—that I cannot possess created things. I cannot touch them, I cannot get into them. They are not my end, I cannot find any rest in them. We who are supposed to be Christians know that well enough, abstractly. Or rather, we say we believe it. Actually, we have to discover it over and over again. We have to experience this truth, with deeper and deeper intensity, as we go on in life. We renounce the pursuit of creatures as ends on certain sacramental occasions. And we return, bit by bit, to our familiarity with them, living as if we had in the world a lasting city.

—The Sign of Jonas

OCTOBER 20

Learn to Meditate

Learn how to meditate on paper. Drawing and writing

are forms of meditation. Learn how to contemplate works of art. Learn how to pray in the streets or in the country. Know how to meditate not only when you have a book in your hand but when you are waiting for a bus or riding on a train. Above all, enter into the Church's liturgy and make the liturgical cycle part of your life—let its rhythm work its way into your body and soul.

—New Seeds of Contemplation

OCTOBER 21

A Life of Ease

Abbot Pastor said: Just as bees are driven out by smoke, and their honey is taken away from them, so a life of ease drives out the fear of the Lord from man's soul and takes away all his good works.

—The Wisdom of the Desert

OCTOBER 22

One Good Place

More and more I appreciate the beauty and the solemnity of the "way" up through the woods, past the barn, up the stony rise, into the grove of tall, straight oaks and hickories around through the pines, swinging to the hilltop and the clearing that looks out over the valley.

Sunrise: hidden by pines and cedars to the east. I saw the red flame of the kingly sun glaring through the black trees; not like dawn, but like a forest fire. Then the sun became distinguished as a person, and he shone silently and with solemn power through the branches, and the whole world was silent and calm.

It is essential to experience all the times and moods of one good place. No one will ever be able to say how essential, how truly part of a genuine life this is; but all this is lost in the abstract, formal routine of exercises under an official fluorescent light.

—Conjectures of a Guilty Bystander

OCTOBER 23

Image and Shadow

The nineteenth-century European and American realists were so realistic that their pictures were totally unlike what they were supposed to represent. And the first thing wrong with them was, of course, precisely that they were pictures. In any case, nothing resembles reality less than the photograph. Nothing resembles substance less than its shadow. To convey the meaning of something substantial, you have to use not a shadow, but a sign; not the imitation, but the image. The image is a new and different reality; and, of course, it does not convey an impression of some object, but the mind of the subject—and that is something else again.

Man is the image of God, not his shadow. At present, we have decided that God is dead and that we are his shadow. Take a picture of that, Jack!

—Conjectures of a Guilty Bystander

OCTOBER 24

A Light Infused

Faith reaches the intellect not simply through the senses but in a light directly infused by God. Since this light does not pass through the eye or the imagination or reason, its certitude becomes our own without any vesture of created appearance, without any likeness that can be visualized or described.

—New Seeds of Contemplation

OCTOBER 25

No New Fires

It is good that I have been out to the common work more often, even though I nearly set the whole forest on fire yesterday burning brush out by Saint Gertrude's field on the slope nearest the lake.

Wind. Flames spring up in the leaves across the creek, like the spread of attachments in an unmortified soul!

So, *confortetur cor tuum et viriliter age!* Here are the things to be done:

Many lights are burning that ought to be put out.

Kindle no new fires. Live in the warmth of the sun.

—The Sign of Jonas

OCTOBER 26

A Turning Point

Meanwhile, autumn is setting in, and the wind is swinging the long branches of the weeping willow behind the chapel, on the way down to the woodshed. As the branches swing, curtains open on to the fall woods and the sheep barn. Everything is rusty, woods and barn together!

So I, too, come to a turning-point of some sort, not knowing yet what it is. I am nearly forty-eight. I have work to do: to get free within myself, to work my way out of the cords and habits of thought, the garments of skins (as if I could do that by myself). But one must want to begin.

—*Conjectures of a Guilty Bystander*

OCTOBER 27
A Shared Holiness

A saint is not so much a man who realizes that he possesses virtues and sanctity as one who is overwhelmed by the sanctity of God. God is holiness. And therefore things are holy in proportion as they share in his being, but men are called to be holy in a far superior way—by somehow sharing his transcendence and rising above the level of everything that is not God.

—*The Sign of Jonas*

OCTOBER 28
Chuang Tzu's Funeral

When Chuang Tzu was about to die, his disciples began planning a splendid funeral.

But he said: "I shall have heaven and earth for my coffin; the sun and moon will be the jade symbols hanging by my side; planets and constellations will shine as jewels all around me, and all beings will be present as mourners at the wake. What more is needed? Everything is amply taken care of!"

But they said: "We fear that crows and kites will eat our Master."

"Well," said Chuang Tzu, "above ground I shall be eaten by crows and kites, below it by ants and worms. In either case, I shall be eaten. Why are you so partial to birds?"

—*The Way of Chuang Tzu*

OCTOBER 29

The Irreligious Mind

The completely irreligious mind is, it seems to me, the unreal mind, the tense, void, abstracted mind that does not even see the things that grow out of the earth or feel glad about them: it knows the world only through prices and figures and statistics. For when the world is reduced to number and measure, you can indeed be irreligious, unless your numbers turn out to be implicated in music, or astronomy, and then the fatal drive to adoration begins again!

The numbers that are germane to music and astronomy are implicated in the magic of seasons and harvests. And there, despite yourself, you recapture something of the hidden and forgotten atavistic joy of those Neolithic peoples who, for whole millennia, were quiet and human.

—Conjectures of a Guilty Bystander

OCTOBER 30

The Time of Darkness

When the time comes to enter the darkness in which we are naked and helpless and alone; in which we see the insufficiency of our greatest strength and the hollowness of our strongest virtues; in which we have nothing of our own to rely on, and nothing in our nature to support us, and nothing in the world to guide us or give us light—then we find out whether or not we live by faith.

—New Seeds of Contemplation

OCTOBER 31

Waters of Contemplation

Call it wine, if you like, or call it water. It comes to the same thing. For there is intoxication in the waters of contemplation, whose mystery fascinated and delighted the first Cistercians and whose image found its way into the names of so many of those valley monasteries that stood in forests, on the banks of clean streams, among rocks alive with springs.

These are the waters which the world does not know, because it prefers the water of bitterness and contradiction. These are the waters of peace, of which Christ said: "He that shall drink of the water that I shall give him, shall not thirst forever. But the water that I shall give him shall become in him a fountain of water, springing up into life everlasting." These are the Waters of Siloe, that flow in silence.

—The Waters of Siloe

An Obscurity So Obscure

The way to contemplation is an obscurity so obscure that it is no longer even dramatic. There is nothing in it that can be grasped and cherished as heroic or even unusual. And so, for a contemplative, there is supreme value in the ordinary everyday routine of work, poverty, hardship, and monotony that characterize the lives of all the poor, uninteresting, and forgotten people in the world.

—New Seeds of Contemplation

November

NOVEMBER 1

In Another Country

Bare woods and driving rain. There was a strong wind. When I reached the hilltop, I found there was something terrible about the landscape. But it was marvelous. The completely unfamiliar aspect of the forest beyond our rampart unnerved me.

It was as though I were in another country. I saw the steep, savage hills covered with black woods and half buried in the storm that was coming at me from the southwest. And the ridges traveled away from this center in unexpected directions. I said, "Now you are indeed alone. Be prepared to fight the devil." But it was not the time of combat. I started down the hill again feeling that perhaps, after all, I had climbed it uselessly.

Halfway down, in a place of comparative shelter, just before the pines begin, I found a bower God had prepared for me, like Jonas's ivy. It had been designed especially for this moment. There was a tree stump in an even place. It was dry and a small cedar arched over it, like a green tent, forming an alcove. There I sat in silence and loved the wind in the forest and listened for a good while to God.

—*The Sign of Jonas*

NOVEMBER 2

All Souls' Day

Some seem to want to make All Souls' Day a feast of death, with such rattling of bones and many skulls. The cult of cemeteries, not as places where bodies sleep in peace awaiting the Resurrection, but where they lie and rot, eaten by worms. In this cult of death, more than anywhere else, there is danger of the universal vulgarity and stupidity of middle-class culture corrupting the Christian spirit. Money has a lot to do with this. The disposal of dead bodies is a lucrative and scandalous business—scandalous in the way sorrow is exploited and insulted with small, unctuous, frightful, utterly useless, and expensive toys. The paint, the cushions, the things that light up, the things that play music.

—*Conjectures of a Guilty Bystander*

NOVEMBER 3

A Good Time to Die

I used to think it would be a good thing to die young and die quickly, but now I am beginning to think a long life with much labor and suffering for God would be the greater grace. However, the greater grace for each individual is the one God wills for him. If God wills you to die suddenly, that is a greater grace for you than any other death, because it is the one he has chosen, by his love, with all the circumstances of your life and his glory in view.

—*The Sign of Jonas*

NOVEMBER 4

In the Himalayas

In the afternoon I got my first real taste of the Himalayas. I climbed a road out of the village up into the mountains, winding through pines, past places where Tibetans live and work. Many Tibetans on the road, and some were at work on a house, singing their building song. Finally, I was out alone in the pines, watching the clouds clear from the medium peaks—but not the high snowy ones—and the place filled with a special majestic kind of mountain silence.

At one point, the sound of a goatherd's flute drifted up from a pasture below. An unforgettable valley with a river winding at the bottom, a couple of thousand feet below, and the rugged peaks above me, and pines twisted as in Chinese paintings. I got on a little path where I met at least five Tibetans silently praying with rosaries in their hands—and building little piles of stones. An Indian goatherd knocked over one of the piles for no reason.

Great silence of the mountain, except for two men with axes higher up in the pines. Gradually, the clouds thinned before one of the higher peaks, but it never fully appeared.

—The Asian Journal of Thomas Merton

NOVEMBER 5

Every Man Alone

Every man is a solitary, held firmly by the inexorable limitations of his own aloneness. Death makes this very clear, for when a man dies, he dies alone. The only one for whom the bell tolls, in all literal truth, is the one who is dying. It tolls "for thee" insofar as death is common to all of us, but obviously we do not all die at one and the same moment. We die like one another. The presence of many living men around the deathbed of one who is in agony may unite them all in the mystery of death, but it also unites them in a mystery of living solitude. It paradoxically unites them while reminding them acutely—and beyond words— of their isolation. Each one will have to die, and die alone. And, at the same time (but this is what they do not want to see), each one must also live alone.

—Disputed Questions

NOVEMBER 6
The Insatiable Shadow

The ambitious run day and night in pursuit of honors, constantly in anguish about the success of their plans, dreading the miscalculation that may wreck everything. Thus they are alienated from themselves, exhausting their real life in service of the shadow created by their insatiable hope.

—*The Way of Chuang Tzu*

NOVEMBER 7
The Inescapable Specters

Man is ever face to face with the inescapable specters of boredom, futility, and madness. A healthy and well-organized social life enables man to cope with these specters by fruitful work, love, and personal growth. The person who loves his ordinary life because his work is meaningful and because his relationship with those around him is joyful, open, and generous will never be bored. An unhealthy social system both exacerbates man's fear of boredom and exploits it. The modern American is kept in terror of boredom and unfulfillment because he is constantly being reminded of their imminence—in order that he may be induced to do something that will exorcise him for the next half hour. Then the terror will rise up again and he will have to buy something else, or turn another switch, or open another bottle, or swallow another pill, or stick himself with a needle in order to keep from collapsing.

—*Contemplation in a World of Action*

NOVEMBER 8
The Greatest Happiness

My opinion is that you never find happiness until you stop looking for it. My greatest happiness consists precisely in doing nothing whatever that is calculated to obtain happiness; and this, in the minds of most people, is the worst possible course.

—*The Way of Chuang Tzu*

NOVEMBER 9
A Sense of Direction

The real function of discipline is not to provide us with maps, but to sharpen our own sense of direction so that when we really get going we can travel without maps.

—*Contemplation in a World of Action*

NOVEMBER 10
Our Smiles Are Symptoms

Our times manifest in us a basic distortion, a deep-rooted moral disharmony against which laws, sermons, philosophies, authority, inspiration, creativity, and apparently even love itself, would seem to have no power. On the contrary, if man turns in desperate hope to all these things, they seem to leave him emptier, more frustrated, and more anguished than ever before. Our sickness is the sickness of disordered love, of the self-love that realizes itself simultaneously to be self-hate and instantly becomes a source of universal, indiscriminate destructiveness.

This is the other side of the coin that was current in the nineteenth century: the belief in indefinite progress, in the supreme goodness of man and of all his appetites. What passes for optimism, even Christian optimism, is the indefectible hope that eighteenth and nineteenth-century attitudes can continue valid, can be kept valid just by the determination to smile, even though the whole world may fall to pieces. Our smiles are symptoms of the sickness.

—*Conjectures of a Guilty Bystander*

NOVEMBER 11

The Politics of Death

In moments that appear to be lucid, I tell myself that in times like these there has to be something for which one is willing to get shot, and for which, in all probability, one is actually going to get shot. What is this? A principle? Faith? Virtue? God? The question is not easy to answer, and maybe it has no answer that can be put into words. Perhaps this is no longer something communicable, or even thinkable. To be executed today (and death by execution is not at all uncommon) one has no need to commit a political crime, to express opposition to a tyrant, or even to hold an objectionable opinion. Indeed, most political deaths under tyrannical regimes are motiveless, arbitrary, absurd. You are shot, or beaten to death, or starved, or worked until you drop, not because of anything you have done, not because of anything you believe in, not because of anything you stand for, but arbitrarily: your death is demanded by something or someone undefined. Your death is necessary to give apparent meaning to a meaningless political process which you have never quite managed to understand.

—*Conjectures of a Guilty Bystander*

NOVEMBER 12

Holy Reformers

Nothing is more suspicious, in a man who seems holy, than an impatient desire to reform other men. Pay as little attention as you can to the faults of other people and none at all to their natural defects and eccentricities.

—New Seeds of Contemplation

NOVEMBER 13

A Contrary Identity

I do not consider myself integrated in the war-making society in which I live, but the problem is that this society does consider me integrated in it. I notice that for nearly twenty years my society—or those in it who read my books—have decided upon an identity for me and insist that I continue to correspond perfectly to the idea of me which they found upon reading my first successful book. Yet the same people simultaneously prescribe for me a contrary identity.

They demand that I remain forever the superficially pious, rather rigid and somewhat narrow-minded young monk I was twenty years ago, and at the same time they continually circulate the rumor that I have left my monastery. What has actually happened is that I have been simply living where I am and developing in my own way without consulting the public about it, since it is none of the public's business.

—Raids on the Unspeakable

NOVEMBER 14

Sales Resistance

If we are fools enough to remain at the mercy of the people who want to sell us happiness, it will be impossible for us ever to be content with anything. How would they profit if we became content? We would no longer need their new product. The last thing the salesman wants is for the buyer to become content. You are of no use in our affluent society unless you are always just about to grasp what you never have.

—*Conjectures of a Guilty Bystander*

NOVEMBER 15

Illusions

How many people there are in the world of today who have "lost their faith" along with the vain hopes and illusions of their childhood. What they called "faith" was just one among all the other illusions. They placed all their hope in a certain sense of spiritual peace, of comfort, of interior equilibrium, of self-respect. Then, when they began to struggle with the real difficulties and burdens of mature life, when they became aware of their own weakness, they lost their peace, they let go of their precious self-respect, and it became impossible for them to "believe." That is to say, it became impossible for them to comfort themselves, to reassure themselves, with the images and concepts that they found reassuring in childhood.

—*New Seeds of Contemplation*

NOVEMBER 16

Obedient to Reason and Grace

Passion and emotion certainly have their place in the life of prayer—but they must be purified, ordered, brought into submission to the highest love. Then they too can share in the spirit's joy and even, in their own small way, contribute to it. But until they are spiritually mature, the passions must be treated firmly and with reserve, even in the "consolations" of prayer. When are they spiritually mature? When they are pure, clean, gentle, quiet, nonviolent, forgetful of themselves, detached and, above all, when they are humble and obedient to reason and to grace.

—*New Seeds of Contemplation*

NOVEMBER 17

The Cosmic Dance

When we are alone on a starlit night, when by chance we see the migrating birds in autumn descending on a grove of junipers to rest and eat; when we see children in a moment when they are really children, when we know love in our own hearts; or when, like the Japanese poet, Basho, we hear an old frog land in a quiet pond with a solitary splash—at such times the awakening, the turning inside out of all values, the "newness," the emptiness and the purity of vision that make themselves evident, all these provide a glimpse of the cosmic dance.

—*New Seeds of Contemplation*

NOVEMBER 18

The World and Time

. . . For the world and time are the dance of the Lord in emptiness. The silence of the spheres is the music of a wedding feast. The more we persist in misunderstanding the phenomena of life, the more we analyze them out into strange finalities and complex purposes of our own, the more we involve ourselves in sadness, absurdity, and despair. But it does not matter much, because no despair of ours can alter the reality of things, or stain the joy of the cosmic dance which is always there. Indeed, we are in the midst of it, and it is in the midst of us, for it beats in our very blood, whether we want it to or not.

—New Seeds of Contemplation

NOVEMBER 19

Once Again Made Clean

My God, who is like you? How can I compare the visits of your children with the silence that dwells on the hills? Yet I have made their hearts suffer by loving them. I have defiled many lives with my impertinence. We have all gone away and have begun over and over to pray, and I believe conversation is a punishment for false mysticism. How can we help ourselves? But I am once again made clean by frost and morning air, here in the presence of the moon.

—The Sign of Jonas

NOVEMBER 20

Pure Morning Light

Outside the dirty window I have just opened, there is pure morning light on the lower rampart of the Himalayas. Near me are the steep green sinews of a bastion tufted with vegetation. A hut or shrine is visible, outlines on the summit. Beyond, in the sunlit, black-lighted mist, the higher pointed peak. Further to the left, a still higher snowy peak that was hidden in the cloud last evening and is misty now. Song of birds in the bushes. Incessant soft guttural mantras of the crows. Below, in another cottage, an argument of women. A white butterfly appears in the sun, then vanishes again. Another passes in the distance. No gain for them—or for me. Down in the valley a bird sings, a boy whistles. The white butterfly zigzags across the top left corner of the view. Cocks crow in the valley. The tall illuminated grasses bend in the wind. One white butterfly hovers and settles. Another passes in a hurry. How glad I am not to be in any city.

—The Asian Journal of Thomas Merton

NOVEMBER 21

Grateful Convictions

How glad, how grateful men are when they can learn from one another what they have already determined, in their hearts, to believe for themselves.

—Conjectures of a Guilty Bystander

NOVEMBER 22

Funnier Than We Think

It is beautifully cool and, above all, quiet in the novitiate conference room. One of the novices, Frater B——, laughed and laughed more and more, week after week, until he finally laughed all day long and had to go home. I am told that once, before one of the singing classes, he laughed so much he rolled on the floor. Life here is funnier than we think. And now it is, once again, quiet.

—Conjectures of a Guilty Bystander

NOVEMBER 23

A Desperate Need

Man is most human, and most proves his humanity (I did not say his virility), by the quality of his relationship with woman. This obsession with virility and conquest makes a true and deep relationship impossible. Men today think that there is no difference between the capacity to make conquests and the capacity to love. Women respond accordingly, with the elaborate deceit and thinly veiled harlotry—the role assigned to women by fashion—and there is a permanent battle between the sexes, sometimes covered over with the most atrocious and phony play acting. In all this everyone completely forgets the need for love. A desperate need: not the need to receive it only, but the need to give love.

—Conjectures of a Guilty Bystander

NOVEMBER 24

Pragmatically Clever

The concept of "virtue" does not appeal to men, because they are no longer interested in becoming good. Yet if you tell them that Saint Thomas talks about virtues as "habits of the practical intellect," they may, perhaps, pay some attention to you. They are pleased with the thought of anything that would seem to make them clever. It gets them something.

—*New Seeds of Contemplation*

NOVEMBER 25

They Made No History

In the age when life on earth was full, no one paid any special attention to worthy men, nor did they single out the man of ability. Rulers were simply the highest branches on the tree, and the people were like deer in the woods. They were honest and righteous without realizing that they were "doing their duty." They loved each other and did not know that this was "love of neighbor." They deceived no one, yet they did not know that they were "men to be trusted." They were reliable and did not know that this was "good faith." They lived freely together, giving and taking, and did not know that they were generous. For this reason their deeds have not been narrated. They made no history.

—*The Way of Chuang Tzu*

November 26

Along with Angels

It was raining and there was a wind. I went to the wagon shed. You could still see the hills in the distance, not too much rain for that—many black clouds, low and torn, like smoke from a disaster, flying angrily over the wide open ruin of the old horsebarn, where I now love to walk alone. On sunny days it does not have this Castle of Otranto look about it. Today, first I was full of a melody that might have been related to something in Stravinsky's "Firebird," which I have nevertheless forgotten. This was mostly my own and I sang it to God, along with angels. Then the melody went away and I sat on a stone.

—*The Sign of Jonas*

November 27

Questions Already Answered

Why should I worry about losing a bodily life that I must inevitably lose anyway, as long as I possess a spiritual life and identity that cannot be lost against my desire? Why should I fear to cease to be what I am not, when I have already become something of what I am? Why should I go to great labor to possess satisfactions that cannot last an hour, and which bring misery after them, when I already own God in his eternity of joy?

—*New Seeds of Contemplation*

NOVEMBER 28

Thanksgiving

Behind the horsebarn after dinner, I made my thanksgiving. The little clouds were beautiful. The sun on the grass was beautiful. Even the ground seemed alive.

Walking along the fence of the new vineyard after Benediction, I looked at the dim full moon and the bare brown woods on the far side of the bottoms, where our neighbor built that little wooden house last summer. It is the only house we can see in that direction or, in fact, in any other. But what I wanted to say was that I don't think I like to walk in the fields with clothes smelling of incense.

—*The Sign of Jonas*

NOVEMBER 29

A Space of Liberty

The contemplative life must provide an area, a space of liberty, of silence, in which possibilities are allowed to surface and new choices—beyond routine choice—become manifest. It should create a new experience of time, not as a stopgap, stillness, but as "tempis vierge"—not a blank to be filled or an untouched space to be conquered and violated, but a space which can enjoy its own potentialities and hopes —and its own presence to itself. One's own time. But not dominated by one's own ego and its demands. Hence open to others—compassionate time, rooted in the sense of common illusion and in criticism of it.

—*The Asian Journal of Thomas Merton*

NOVEMBER 30

Advent in Gethsemani

It is important to remember the deep, in some ways anguished, seriousness of Advent, when the mendacious celebrations of our marketing culture so easily harmonize with our tendency to regard Christmas, consciously or otherwise, as a return to our own innocence and our own infancy. Advent should remind us that the "King Who is to come" is more than a charming infant smiling (or, if you prefer, a dolorous spirituality, weeping) in the straw. There is certainly nothing wrong with the traditional family joys of Christmas, nor need we be ashamed to find ourselves still able to anticipate them without too much ambivalence. After all, that in itself is no mean feat.

—*Seasons of Celebration*

Advent in Ceylon

It is hardly like any Advent I have ever known! A clear, hot sky. Flowering trees. A hot day coming. I woke at the sound of many crows fighting in the air. Then the booming drum at the Temple of Buddha's Tooth. Now, the traffic of buses, and a cool breeze sways the curtains. The jungle is very near, it comes right to the top of the city and is visible a bare hundred yards from this window.

—*The Asian Journal of Thomas Merton*

December

DECEMBER 1

A Door Opens

A door opens in the center of our being and we seem to fall through it into immense depths which, although they are infinite, are all accessible to us; all eternity seems to have become ours in this one placid and breathless contact.

God touches us with a touch that is emptiness, and empties us. He moves us with a simplicity that simplifies us. All variety, all complexity, all paradox, all multiplicity cease. Our mind swims in the air of an understanding, a reality that is dark and serene and includes in itself everything. Nothing more is desired. Nothing more is wanting. Our only sorrow, if sorrow be possible at all, is the awareness that we ourselves still live outside of God.

For already a supernatural instinct teaches us that the function of this abyss of freedom, which has been opened out within our own midst, is to draw us utterly out of our own selfhood and into its own immensity of liberty and joy.

—*New Seeds of Contemplation*

DECEMBER 2

The Stranger Is Ourselves

We have come to the end of a long journey and see that the stranger we meet there is no other than ourselves—which is the same as saying that we find Christ in him.

—*Mystics and Zen Masters*

December 3
Sweet Point of Dawn

The most wonderful moment of the day is when creation, in its innocence, asks permission to "be" once again, as it did on the first morning that ever was.

All wisdom seeks to collect and manifest itself at that blind sweet point. Man's wisdom does not succeed, for we are fallen into self-mastery and cannot ask permission of anyone. We face our mornings as men of undaunted purpose. We know the time and we dictate terms. We have a clock that proves we are right from the very start. We know what time it is.

For the birds there is not a time that they tell, but the virgin point between darkness and light, between nonbeing and being. The waking of crows is most like the waking of men: querulous, noisy, raw.

Here is an unspeakable secret: paradise is all around us and we do not understand. It is wide open. The sword is taken away, but we do not know it: we are off "one to his farm and another to his merchandise." Lights on. Clocks ticking. Thermostats working. Stoves cooking. Electric shavers filling radios with static. "Wisdom," cries the dawn deacon, but we do not attend.

—*Conjectures of a Guilty Bystander*

December 4
The Joy of Unimportance

I think the chief reason why we have so little joy is that we take ourselves too seriously. Joy can only be real if it is based on truth, and since the fall of Adam all man's life is shot through with falsehood and illusion. That is why Saint Bernard is right in leading us back to joy by the love of truth. His starting-point is the truth of our own insignificance in comparison with God. To penetrate the truth of how utterly unimportant we are is the only thing that can set us free to enjoy true happiness.

—The Sign of Jonas

DECEMBER 5
The Certainty of Hope

The certainty of Christian hope lies beyond passion and beyond knowledge. Therefore, we must sometimes expect our hope to come in conflict with darkness, desperation and ignorance. Therefore, too, we must remember that Christian optimism is not a perpetual sense of euphoria, an indefectible comfort in whose experience neither anguish nor tragedy can possibly exist. We must not strive to maintain a clime of optimism by the mere suppression of tragic realities. Christian optimism lies in a hope of victory that transcends all tragedy: a victory in which we pass beyond tragedy to glory with Christ crucified and risen.

—Seasons of Celebration

DECEMBER 6
When Holiness Seems Natural

It is beautiful to see God's grace working in people. The most beautiful thing about it is to see how the desires of the soul, inspired by God, so fit in and harmonize with grace that holy things seem natural to the soul, seem to be part of its very self. That is what God wants to create in us—that marvelous spontaneity in which his life becomes perfectly ours and our life his, and it seems inborn in us to act as his children, and to have his light shining out of our eyes.

—*The Sign of Jonas*

DECEMBER 7
Nearing the End

We are all nearing the end of our work. The night is falling upon us, and we find ourselves without the serenity and fulfillment that were the lot of our fathers. I do not think this is necessarily a sign that anything is lacking, but rather is to be taken as a greater incentive to trust more fully in the mercy of God, and to advance further into his mystery. Our faith can no longer serve merely as a happiness pill. It has to be the Cross and the resurrection of Christ. And this it will be, for all of us who so desire.

—*Seeds of Destruction*

DECEMBER 8
Life in Wisdom

Our full spiritual life is life in wisdom, life in Christ. The darkness of faith bears fruit in the light of wisdom.

—*New Seeds of Contemplation*

DECEMBER 9
I Saw a City

I dreamt I was lost in a great city and was walking "toward

the center" without quite knowing where I was going. Suddenly, I came to a dead end, but on a height, looking at a great bay, an arm of the harbor. I saw a whole section of the city spread out before me on hills covered with light snow, and realized that, though I had far to go, I knew where I was: because in this city there are two arms of the harbor and they help you to find your way, as you are always encountering them.

Then, in this city, I speak with a stranger in the library (being still on my way). I realize that there is a charterhouse here, and that I have been meaning to go there, to speak to the prior about my vocation. I ask "where is the charterhouse?" He says: "I am just going to drive that way, and I go right by it. I will take you." I accept his offer, realizing that it is providential.

—Conjectures of a Guilty Bystander

DECEMBER 10
In the Presence of Possibility

I think sometimes that I may soon die, though I am not yet old (forty-seven). I don't know exactly what kind of conviction this thought carries with it or what I mean by it. Death is always a possibility for everyone. We live in the presence of this possibility. So I have a habitual awareness that I may die, and that if this is God's will, then I am glad. "Go ye forth to meet Him," and in the light of this I realize the futility of my cares and preoccupations, particularly my chief care, which is central to me, my work as a writer.

I do not feel very guilty about it, but it remains a "care," a focus that keeps my "self" in view, and I feel a little hampered. Though I know by experience that without this care and salutary work I would be much more in my own way, much more obstructed by my own inertia and confusion. If I am not fully free, then the love of God, I hope, will free me. The important thing is simply turning to him daily and after, preferring his will and his mystery to everything that is evidently and tangibly "mine."

—*Conjectures of a Guilty Bystander*

DECEMBER 11

Man's Sorrow

The birth of a man is the birth of his sorrow.

The longer he lives, the more stupid he becomes, because his anxiety to avoid unavoidable death becomes more and more acute. What bitterness! He lives for what is always out of reach! His thirst for survival in the future makes him incapable of living in the present.

—*The Way of Chuang Tzu*

DECEMBER 12

When Night Comes

This idea of a "writing career" which begins somewhere and ends somewhere is also a beautifully stupid fiction. . . . And I don't feel that my days as a writer are over. I don't care where they are. The point for me is that I must stop trying to adjust myself to the fact that night will come and the work will end. So night comes. Then what? You sit in the dark. What is wrong with that? Meanwhile, it is time to give to others whatever I have to give and not reflect on it. I wish I had learned the knack of doing this without question or care. Perhaps I can begin. It is not a matter of adjustment or of peace. It is a matter of truth, and patience, and humility. Stop trying to "adjust."

Adjust to what? To the general fiction?

—Conjectures of a Guilty Bystander

DECEMBER 13

The Society of Zero

All has been leveled to equal meaninglessness. But it is not quite the same. It is not that all is "one," but all is "zero." Everything adds up to zero. Indeed, even the state, in the end, is zero. Freedom is then to live and die for zero. Is that what I want: to be beaten, imprisoned, or shot for zero? But to be shot for zero is not a matter of choice. It is not something one is required either to "want" or "not want." It is not even something one is able to foresee.

Zero swallows hundreds of thousands of victims every year, and the police take care of the details. Suddenly, mysteriously, without reason, your time comes, and while you are still desperately trying to make up your own mind what you imagine you might possibly be dying for, you are swallowed up by zero. Perhaps, subjectively, you have tried to convince yourself and have not wasted time convincing others. Nobody else is interested. What I have said so far concerns execution for a "political crime." But death in war, in the same way, is a kind of execution for nothing, a meaningless extinction, a swallowing up by zero.

—Conjectures of a Guilty Bystander

DECEMBER 14

Ambition and Silence

There is nothing on this earth that does not give me a pain. Conversation in town, ambition in the cloister: I mean even ambition to do great things for God. That ambition is too much like the ambitions of the town.

I am aware of silence all around me in the country as of a world that is closed to men. They live in it and yet its door is closed to them. This silence, it is everywhere. It is the room Jesus told us to enter into when we pray.

—The Sign of Jonas

DECEMBER 15
After the Night Office

I listen to the clock tick. Downstairs the thermostat has just stopped humming. God is in this room. So much so that it is difficult to read or write. Nevertheless, I'll get busy on Isaias, which is your word, O my God, and may your fire grow in me and may I find you in your beautiful fire. It is very quiet, O my God, your moon shines on our hills. Your moonlight shines in my wide open soul when everything is silent.

—The Sign of Jonas

To Be Created

The poet enters into himself in order to create. The contemplative enters into God in order to be created.

—New Seeds of Contemplation

DECEMBER 16
Suspended in Air

"Vacio, hambriento, solo, ilagado y doliente de amor, sus-

penso en el aire" ("Empty, famished, alone, wounded and suffering with love, suspended in the air!").

Walking back from the barns in the warm sun on the muddy road between the orchard and the vegetable garden, with the *Spiritual Canticle* under my arm, and saying those wonderful words! I found a fine place to read and pray, on the top floor of that barn building where the rabbits used to be. Up under the roof is a place reached by various ladders. Some stovepipes and old buckets are there and many of the little boxes in which the novices gather strawberries in the early summertime. There is a chair and there is a beautiful small rectangular window which faces south over the valley —the further orchard, Saint Joseph's field, the distant line of hills. It is the quietest and most hidden and most isolated place I have found in the whole enclosure—but not necessarily the warmest. However, it was good yesterday with the sun coming in the window: *"Vacio, hambriento, solo, ilagado y doliente de amor, suspenso en el aire"* . . . I sink into deep peace, recollection, and happiness.

—*The Sign of Jonas*

DECEMBER 17

The Sleeper's Response

Many of the Zen stories, which are almost always incomprehensible in rational terms, are simply the ringing of an alarm clock, and the reaction of the sleeper. Usually, the misguided sleeper makes a response which in effect turns off the alarm so that he can go back to sleep. Sometimes he jumps out of bed with a shout of astonishment that it is so late. Sometimes he just sleeps and does not hear the alarm at all.

—*Zen and the Birds of Appetite*

DECEMBER 18

The Unknown Self

Gabriel Marcel says that the artist who labors to produce effects for which he is well-known is unfaithful to himself. This may seem obvious enough when it is badly stated: but how differently we act. We are all too ready to believe that the self we have created out of our more or less inauthentic efforts to be real in the eyes of others is a "real self." We even take it for our identity. Fidelity to such a nonidentity is, of course, infidelity to our real person, which is hidden in mystery. Who will you find that has enough faith and self-respect to attend to this mystery and to begin by accepting himself as unknown? God help the man who thinks he knows all about himself.

—*Conjectures of a Guilty Bystander*

DECEMBER 19

The Scar That Burns

When God allows us to fall back into our own confusion of desires and judgments and temptations, we carry a scar over the place where that joy exulted for a moment in our hearts.

The scar burns us. The sore wound aches within us, and we remember that we have fallen back into what we are not, and are not yet allowed to remain where God would have us belong. We long for the place he had destined for us, and weep with desire for the time when his pure poverty will catch us and hold us in its liberty and never let us go, when we will never fall back from the Paradise of the simple and the little children into the forum of prudence, where the wise of this world go up and down in sorrow and set their traps for a happiness that cannot exist.

—*New Seeds of Contemplation*

DECEMBER 20

Obscurity of Faith

The very obscurity of faith is an argument of its perfection. It is darkness to our minds because it so far transcends their weakness. The more perfect the faith is, the darker it becomes. The closer we get to God, the less is our faith diluted with the half-light of created images and concepts.

—*New Seeds of Contemplation*

The Fullness of Grace

I am the utter poverty of God. I am His emptiness, littleness, nothingness, lostness. When this is understood, my life in His freedom, the self-emptying of God in me is the fullness of grace. A love for God that knows no reason because He is the fullness of grace. A love for God that knows no reason because He is God; a love without measure, a love for God as personal. The Ishvara appears as personal in order to inspire his love. Love for all, hatred of none is the fruit and manifestation of love for God—peace and satisfaction. Forgetfulness of worldly pleasure, selfishness and so on in the love for God, channeling all passion and emotion into love for God.

—*Woods, Shore, Desert*

DECEMBER 21
Simple and Free

To belong to God I have to belong to myself. I have to be alone—at least interiorly alone. This means the constant renewal of a decision. I cannot belong to people. None of me belongs to anybody but God. Absolute loneliness of the imagination, the memory, the will. My love for everybody is equal, neutral, and clean. No exclusiveness. Simple and free as the sky, because I love everybody and am possessed by nobody, not held, not bound.

In order to be not remembered or even wanted, I have to be a person that nobody knows. They can have Thomas Merton. He's dead. Father Louis—he's half dead too. For my part, my name is that sky, those fence-posts, and those cedar trees. I shall not even reflect on who I am and I shall not say my identity is nobody's business, because that implies a truculence I don't intend. It has no meaning. . . . Now my whole life is this—to keep unencumbered. The wind owns the fields where I walk and I own nothing and am owned by nothing, and I shall never even be forgotten because no one will ever discover me.

—*The Sign of Jonas*

DECEMBER 22
The Magnifying Glass

As a magnifying glass concentrates the rays of the sun into a little burning knot of heat that can set fire to a dry leaf or a piece of paper, so the mystery of Christ in the Gospel concentrates the rays of God's light to a point that sets fire to the spirit of man.

—New Seeds of Contemplation

DECEMBER 23

Attuned to the Cosmos

Very cold morning, about 8° above. I left for the woods before dawn . . . Pure dark sky, with only the crescent moon and planets shining.

Sunrise is an event that calls forth solemn music in the very depths of man's nature, as if one's whole being had to attune itself to the cosmos and praise God for the new day, praise him in the name of all the creatures that ever were or ever will be.

I look at the rising sun and feel that now upon me falls the responsibility of seeing what all my ancestors have seen, in the Stone Age and even before it, praising God before me. Whether or not they praised him then, for themselves, they must praise him now in me. When the sun rises, each one of us is summoned by the living and the dead to praise God.

—Conjectures of a Guilty Bystander

DECEMBER 24

Mary, the Window of God

Mary, who was empty of all egotism, free from all sin, was as pure as the glass of a very clean window that has no other function than to admit the light of the sun. If we rejoice in that light, we implicitly praise the cleanness of the window. And, of course, it might be argued that in such a case we might well forget the window altogether. This is true. And yet the Son of God, in emptying himself of his majestic power, having become a child, abandoning himself in complete dependence to the loving care of a human mother, in a certain sense draws our attention once again to her. The Light has wished to remind us of the window, because he is grateful to her and because he has an infinitely tender and personal love for her. If he asks us to share this love, it is certainly a great grace and a privilege, and one of the most important aspects of this privilege is that it enables us, to some extent, to appreciate the mystery of God's great love and respect for his creatures.

—New Seeds of Contemplation

The Light

The Light in which we are one does not change.

—Seeds of Destruction

DECEMBER 25

Nativity Kerygma

Christ, light of light, is born today, and since he is born to us, he is born in us as light, and therefore we who believe are born today to new light. That is to say, our souls are born to new life and new grace by receiving him who is the truth. For Christ, invisible in his own nature, has become visible in our nature. What else can this mean, except that first he has become visible as man; and secondly, he has become visible in his Church? He wills to be visible in us, to live in us, work in us, and save us through his secret action in our own hearts and the hearts of our brothers. So we must receive the light of the newborn Savior by faith, in order to manifest it by our witness in common praise and by the works of our charity towards one another.

We are born in Christ today. . . . Can it be surprising that we feel in our hearts the exultation of the divine light which streams into our spirit from the presence of the newborn Savior and transforms us from glory to glory in his image? This is the mystery of light which shines upon us today.

—Seasons of Celebration

DECEMBER 26

Hagia Sophia

Hagia Sophia in all things is the Divine Life reflected in them, considered as a spontaneous participation, as their invitation to the wedding feast.

She is in all things like the air receiving the sunlight. In her they prosper. In her they glorify God. In her they rejoice to reflect Him. In her they are united with Him. She is the union between them. She is the Love that unites them. She is life as communion, life as thanksgiving, life as praise, life as festival, life as glory.

God enters in His creation. Through her wise answer, through her obedient understanding, through the sweet yielding consent of Sophia, God enters without publicity into the city of rapacious men.

She crowns Him not with what is glorious, but with what is greater than glory: the one thing greater than glory is weakness, nothingness, poverty.

The shadows fall. The stars appear. The birds begin to sleep. Night embraces the silent half of the earth. A vagrant, a destitute wanderer with dusty feet, finds his way down a new road. A homeless God, lost in the night, without papers, without identification, without even a number, a frail expendable exile lies down in desolation under the sweet stars of the world and entrusts himself to sleep.

—Emblems for a Season of Fury

DECEMBER 27
Amid Songs of Angels

This Child and Redeemer Who comes amid the songs of angels to answer the prayers of all the Patriarchs and Prophets, and to satisfy the unrecognized longings of the whole lineage of Adam, exiled from Paradise, comes also to quiet the groanings of all creation. For the whole world has been in labor and in mourning since the fall of man. The whole created universe, with all its manifold beauty and splendor, has travailed in disorder, longing for the birth of a Savior. The Patriarchs and Prophets prayed for the coming of Christ in Bethlehem, and this first coming did not silence the groanings of creation.

—Seasons of Celebration

DECEMBER 28
Make Known the Presence

The mystery of Christmas therefore lays upon us all a debt and an obligation to the rest of men and to the whole created universe. We who have seen the light of Christ are obliged, by the greatness of the grace that has been given us, to make known the presence of the Savior to the ends of the earth. This we will do not only by preaching the glad tidings of his coming but, above all, by revealing him in our lives. Christ is born to us . . . in order that he may appear to the whole world through us.

—Seasons of Celebration

DECEMBER 29

Thinking About My Life

Thinking about my own life and future, it is still a very open question. I am beginning to appreciate the hermitage at Gethsemani more than I did last summer, when things seemed so noisy and crowded. Even here in the Himalayas there are few places where one does not run into someone. Roads and paths and trails are all full of people. To have real solitude one would have to get very high up and far back!

Trying to get a better perspective on the earlier part of this year, there is a lot I cannot quite understand. And perhaps do not need to understand. The last months have been demanding and fruitful. I have needed the experience of this journey. Much as the hermitage has meant, I have been needing to get away from Gethsemani, and it was long overdue.

This evening the lights in the cottage went dead for awhile. I stood out in the moonlight, listening to drums down in the village and looking up at the stars. The same constellations as over the hermitage and the porch opening in about the same direction, southeast toward Aquila and the Dolphin. Aquarius out over the plain, the Swan up above. Cassiopeia over the mountains.

—*The Asian Journal of Thomas Merton*

DECEMBER 30

Gethsemani: Night Watch

Now I shall ascend to the top of this religious city, leaving its modern history behind. I climb the trembling, twisted stair into the belfry. The darkness stirs with a flurry of wings high above me in the gloomy engineering that holds the steeple together. Nearer at hand, the old clock ticks in the tower. I flash the light into the mystery which keeps it going, and gaze upon the ancient bells.

And now my whole being breathes the wind which blows through the belfry, and my hand is on the door through which I see the heavens. The door swings out upon a vast sea of darkness and of prayer. Will it come like this, the moment of my death? Will You open a door upon the great forest and set my feet upon a ladder under the moon, and take me out among the stars?

—The Sign of Jonas

DECEMBER 31

Day unto Day

Day unto day uttereth speech. The clouds change. The seasons pass over our woods and fields in their slow and regular procession, and time is gone before you are aware of it. In one sense, we are always traveling, and traveling as if we did not know where we were going. In another sense, we have already arrived.

—The Seven Storey Mountain

Breaking with the Past

But I do have a past to break with, an accumulation of inertia, waste, wrong, foolishness, rot, junk, a great need of clarification of mindfulness, or rather of no mind—a return to genuine practice, right effort, need to push on to the great doubt. Need for the Spirit.

Hang on to the clear light!

—Woods, Shore, Desert

AFTERWORD

Come, let us go into the body of that light. Let us live in the cleanliness of that song. Let us throw off the pieces of the world like clothing and enter into wisdom. For this is what all hearts pray for when they cry: "Thy will be done."

—*New Seeds of Contemplation*

$7.95

A Meditation a Day from Thomas Merton

This convenient day book is a compendium of inspiring passages from the writings of one of this century's spiritual giants. It offers daily challenges for thoughtful meditation intended to stimulate, provoke, and lead to grace. Here are some enduring thoughts found in these pages:

◦◈◦

"We cannot be happy if we expect to live all the time at the highest peak of intensity. Happiness is not a matter of intensity, but of balance and order and rhythm and harmony."

"Every moment and every event of every man's life on earth plants something in his soul."

"Nothing is more suspicious, in a man who seems holy, than an impatient desire to reform other men. Pay as little attention as you can to the faults of other people and none at all to their natural defects and eccentricities."

"The wise heart lives in Christ."

"Wisdom manifests itself, and yet is hidden. The more it hides, the more it is manifest; and the more it is manifest, the more it is hidden. For God is known where he is apprehended as unknown, and he is heard when we realize that we do not know the sound of his voice."

"God utters me like a word containing a partial thought of himself."

"Our full spiritual life is life in wisdom, life in Christ. The darkness of faith bears fruit in the light of wisdom."

"Love cannot come of emptiness. It is full of reality."

◦◈◦

A Doubleday Image Book

COVER PHOTO BY H. ABERNATHY
COURTESY OF H. ARMSTRONG ROBERTS   1085   ISBN: 0-385-23234-9